The COMPLETE
IDIOT'S
GUIDE TO
Winning Through Negotiation

by John Ilich

alpha
books

A Division of Macmillan General Reference
A Simon & Schuster Macmillan Company
1633 Broadway, New York, NY 10019

International Standard Book Number: 0-02-861037-7
Library of Congress Catalog Card Number: 95-083355

98 97 96   8 7 6 5 4 3 2 1

Interpretation of the printing code: the rightmost number of the first series of numbers is the year of the book's printing; the rightmost number of the second series of numbers is the number of the book's printing. For example, a printing code of 96-1 shows that the first printing occurred in 1996.

Printed in the United States of America

Publisher
Theresa Murtha

Editor in Chief
Megan Newman

Development Editor
Jennifer Perillo

Copy/Production Editor
Lynn Northrup

Cover Designer
Michael Freeland

Designer
Kim Scott

Illustrator
Judd Winick

Production Manager
Kelly Dobbs

Production Team Supervisor
Laurie Casey

Production Control Specialists
Jason Hand
Bobbi Satterfield

Indexer
Ginny Bess

Production Team
Heather Butler
Angela Calvert
Kim Cofer
Aleata Howard
Clint Lahnen
Erika Millen
Erich Richter
Scott Tullis
Megan Wade

Contents at a Glance

Contents

Foreword

I assume you've picked up this book because you're facing an important negotiation—whether you're trying to sell your house, ask your boss for a raise, or settle a legal argument. Or, perhaps more importantly, you've turned to this book because you've discovered that each day of your life is filled with situations that require negotiation—getting the kids to keep their curfew, convincing the dry cleaner to press your pants correctly, persuading the telephone company to install a new phone line on time. The skills you learn in *The Complete Idiot's Guide to Winning Through Negotiation* will help you succeed in any type of negotiation, from the most commonplace to the most complex.

Author John Ilich, a lawyer and master negotiator with a 35-year track record, has helped his clients come out on top in a wide range of negotiations. He is also an expert teacher who shares his wisdom throughout the pages of this highly accessible book.

Logical and easy-to-follow, *The Complete Idiot's Guide to Winning Through Negotiation* shows you how to prepare for a negotiation, how to size up your opponent, and how to stay cool and collected when the bargaining gets hot. With John Ilich's guidance, you'll learn how to take control of any negotiation and persuade your opponent to give you what you want. He even tells you what not to do, so you'll avoid the pitfalls that can kill a deal. And best of all, he spices his advice with a wonderful dash of humor.

Don't be fooled by the book's title, though. This is not a guide for novices alone. Even the most sophisticated professional will find helpful suggestions here. I can attest to that personally.

As the owner of a public relations agency and a consultant to other entrepreneurs, I thought I knew a lot about creating win-win bargaining situations. But I quickly discovered as I breezed through this book that there's always more to learn. John Ilich's tactics get results. As soon as I finished reading *The Complete Idiot's Guide to Winning Through Negotiation*, I was able to put the book's advice to work—first while negotiating a major contract for my company, and second by convincing my neighbor to lower the volume on his stereo (something I'd been trying to do for months).

And that's what makes this book so wonderful. You can use John Ilich's insights immediately, in both complicated business situations and everyday life. You don't need any special talents to employ these tactics. All you need to do is hone your skills and understand exactly what happens during the negotiating process. And that's just what John Ilich shows you in plain and simple language, using a format unlike any I've ever seen in other books on negotiation. In addition to worksheets, checklists, and examples that illustrate the author's points, there are extras—sidebars that contain important tips, "Dealbreaker Alerts" that warn you of dangers, quotes from other savvy negotiators, definitions of important terms, and insightful case studies.

It was wise of you to pick up this book, because John Ilich's advice can have a powerful impact on your life. I'm sure you realize that by negotiating better deals for yourself, your business, and your family, you'll make more money and save more too. But that's not all—there are other rewards as well. Good negotiating skills can help you gain a better understanding of human nature. When you learn to negotiate well, without threats and intimidation, without fear and guilt, you'll find that your interactions with other people will go more smoothly and will give you a greater sense of satisfaction. What can be better in life than to get what you want and feel good about it too?

So what are you waiting for? Embrace this book. Profit and enjoy.

Jane Wesman
President of Jane Wesman Public Relations, Inc.
Author of *Dive Right In—The Sharks Won't Bite: The Entrepreneurial Woman's Guide to Success*

Introduction

In one of my earliest experiences as a novice negotiator, back in Chicago some 35 years ago, I faced a couple of old pros who negotiated me into a corner. As we shook hands, they looked me over like hungry lions sizing up a helpless lamb. Then they hauled out all the evidence they had prepared—reports, witness statements, and a truckload of supporting documents. When the discussions began, their language flowed as beautifully as a Shakespearean sonnet. I was outmatched and in awe. I remember thinking, "Wow! Those guys are good—really good! They're major leaguers."

My second reaction was: "I'm going to do whatever it takes to be better than them." From that time on, I dedicated myself to honing my negotiating tips and techniques. Several years later, I negotiated a settlement that saved my client more than nine million dollars. I had arrived. I was a major leaguer.

This is the fifth book on negotiation I've written. I wrote it for you: a person who's not a professional negotiator, yet whose entire life is influenced by negotiation. Think of all the times you've settled disputes with your family, friends, co-workers, clients, or customers. How many times you've bought a car, sold a house, signed a lease, or asked for a raise. Think about how many times you'll do all this again in the future. Wouldn't it be easier if you knew how to bargain like a pro?

The tactics and techniques in this book will help you even when you're not sitting down to a formal bargaining table—like the couple with six young children who were having a new home built. The contractor promised the home would be finished by the summer, when the kids were out of school, but it didn't look like the job would be anywhere near complete by that time. The husband hit on a brilliant solution. He sent the contractor a note: "After June 1st, you will be working for six full-time supervisors under the age of 12." The contractor rushed to complete the job. (The husband was using a simple technique I'll describe in detail in Chapter 19.) That shows you how a little bargaining knowledge can bring you great results!

Like that couple, with the knowledge you gain from this book, you'll know how to handle every situation in which things aren't going your way.

So let's get started. I think you'll like what you read and I *know* you'll benefit from it.

Part 1: The Basics of Successful Negotiation shows you how to prepare for negotiation—how to determine your own position, figure out the other side's bargaining strategy, and arrange the negotiation to give you negotiating power.

Part 2: At the Bargaining Table: Basic Negotiating Techniques lays out the tips and techniques used by master negotiators. You'll discover how to present your case in the most powerful and persuasive way possible—how to use the language of negotiation, how to speak with body language, how to use questions and correspondence as bargaining tools, and more.

Part 3: You and Your Opponent shows you the best ways to appeal to your opponent. You'll learn how to discover negotiating solutions that give both you and your opponent exactly what you want.

Part 4: Increasing Your Negotiating Power explains how you can increase and maintain your personal power in a negotiating situation. You'll learn how to control the negotiating session, conquer bad habits, and use rehearsal to boost your confidence and competence when it comes time to negotiate.

Part 5: Overcoming Problems in Negotiation helps you save a negotiation that has gone awry. Learn how to recoup when fear, anger, or personality or principle conflicts threaten to derail your negotiation.

Part 6: Sealing the Deal helps you cruise through the final stages of negotiation, from making offers and counteroffers to bringing the negotiation to a close.

Part 7: Everyday Negotiating Situations deals with the many common bargaining situations you'll face, such as buying or selling a home, car, or property; negotiating a loan or raise; and bargaining as a consumer.

Extras

In addition to packing this book with pointers, worksheets, checklists, and examples, I've included sidebars that will alert you to important tips, warnings, sayings, case studies, and definitions. Look for these signposts as you read through the text:

Dealmaking Tip
Bargaining tips you can use and profit from when you're at the bargaining table, raring to persuade your opponent to give you what you want.

Dealbreaker Alert
Pitfalls to avoid that can derail your negotiation.

It's Been Said
Aphorisms and quotables that highlight and reinforce basic negotiating truths.

Let's Talk Terms
Basic words and terms in every negotiator's lexicon.

Negotiating Hall of Fame

Case studies of negotiators famous for getting what they want.

Acknowledgments

Special thanks to my wife, Marjorie, for her fine editing assistance.

Special thanks also to the crew at Macmillan Publishing for making this book possible: Theresa Murtha, Megan Newman, Jennifer Perillo, Lynn Northrup, and the entire production team.

Special Thanks from the Publisher

The Complete Idiot's Guide to Winning Through Negotiation was reviewed by an expert in the field who not only checked the technical accuracy of what you'll learn here, but also provided insight to help us ensure that this book gives you everything you need to know to become a successful negotiator. Our special thanks are extended to Sara Adler, a graduate of the University of California at Los Angeles School of Law, and a member of the National Academy of Arbitrators.

Part 1
The Basics of Successful Negotiation

Almost every day of your life, you have to negotiate—sometimes in unexpected ways. What do you do when your car decides not start the day after its warranty expires? Or when you need a loan, but can't afford the high interest rate? When your teenager wants an increased allowance, but hasn't done any chores? Or when you arrive at the airport only to find you've been bumped off your flight?

In all of these situations, you've got three choices. You can surrender and accept the situation without complaint. You can use intimidating bully tactics to try and get what you want. Or you can successfully negotiate.

Like any other art, negotiation has certain basic preparation skills that are easy to learn. A painter, for example, must have a good grasp of colors, paints, brushes, and techniques to paint a picture—and possibly even create a masterpiece. In this part, you learn the basics you need to handle any negotiation—and even negotiate yourself a masterpiece.

Why Learn to Negotiate?

What images come to mind when you think of negotiation? Perhaps a tense room packed with sweaty business people shuffling papers, crunching numbers, and carving out the details of a crucial deal. Maybe a pair of suave diplomats coolly resolving affairs of state over cigars and brandy. Or a fast-talking car salesperson praising the virtues (and sugar-coating the price) of the latest lemon on the lot.

The truth is, negotiation isn't a complicated art best saved for business moguls, union bosses, or international leaders. It's for all people who try to get what they want—and that includes you. In this chapter, I show you the meaning and benefits of successful negotiation.

You're Already a Negotiator

You began your negotiating career the moment you were born and let out your first wail, even though you weren't consciously aware of it. Crying was your way of demanding food or attention or affection. More often than not, you probably succeeded in getting what you wanted.

Let's Talk Terms
Negotiating is a way (often the only way) to get what you want. It's a way to deal with people and to increase your skills in human understanding and interaction. Negotiation is not the same as *manipulation*, in which you use unfair or underhanded means to reach your goals. Negotiation encourages a cooperative relationship, in which both sides want to reach an agreement.

As you got older, your methods of negotiation became more sophisticated—and the results more satisfying. When you were a child, you persuaded your family to buy you toys and give you an allowance. As a teenager, you coaxed privileges from parents and teachers. You also learned how to balance your personality and interests with those of your friends. During all of these experiences, you were trying to get your own way. You were *negotiating*. Successful negotiating simply means knowing how to motivate people to give you what you want.

As an adult, your negotiations are even more serious. Are you thinking of renting an apartment or buying a home? Are you in the market for a car? Do you dream of starting your own business, or would you love to bring home a little more bacon by winning a raise or promotion? The stakes may be higher, but you're still trying to get what you want. You're still negotiating.

The results will always be the same. If you know how to negotiate, you'll enjoy greater success, smoother relationships, and you'll be happier. Since you already are a negotiator, and will be one for the rest of your life, why not perfect your negotiating skills? If you do, you'll reap enormous benefits.

Mo' Money

Some of the best benefits of successful negotiation are those that show up in your paycheck or in your wallet. Once you master the art of wheeling and dealing, you'll discover plenty of opportunities to increase your cash flow—whether by boosting your salary or whittling down the price tags on major purchases.

Make Money—Lots of Money

If you've ever tried to muster up the courage to confront your boss about a raise or promotion, you know how nerve-wracking it can be—and today's streamlined corporate climate doesn't make it any easier. Any kind of discussion about your worth can lead to a knotted stomach, dry throat, and trembling fingers. But once you learn the right approach (which is covered in Chapter 27), you can handle the discussion with cool confidence—and that in itself will boost your chances of getting a raise or promotion.

Likewise, if you're selling your home, car, or property, you'll command top dollar if you know how to negotiate for it.

Save Money—Lots of Money

It's simple: Every time you save money, you make money, and the more you save, the more you make.

I once helped a client buy an $80,000 property for $40,000—half the asking price. Several years later, my client sold the property for $140,000. Thanks to some savvy negotiating, my client was able to make a sweet $100,000 profit.

Another way to increase your wealth is by decreasing your expenses. Every time you buy a car, furniture, clothes, property—anything your heart desires—you'll save money if you know how to negotiate. The money you save can add up to hundreds or even thousands of dollars.

Not only will negotiating a lower price make you richer, it will also give you a wonderful feeling of accomplishment. You'll enjoy your negotiating conquests, your power of persuasion, and your ability to get your way. The victory is especially sweet when you're confronted with difficult situations and the odds are stacked heavily against you.

It's Been Said
"If you would be wealthy, think of saving as well as getting."
—Benjamin Franklin

How to Make Friends and Influence People

Almost every day you try to get your way with those closest to you—your family, friends, and co-workers. Your ability to negotiate can make all these relationships easier.

Family Matters

If your family is anything like mine, I'll bet that every day you find yourself trying to coax those closest to you to do what you want—while your family members are equally determined to watch out for their own interests. In fact, you probably find yourself negotiating at home as often—if not more often—than you do at the office.

Nearly every facet of family life, from deciding who cooks dinner to choosing the ideal vacation spot, involves negotiation. As you hone your negotiating skills, you'll find these everyday discussions becoming a lot easier to handle.

Children can be especially tough to negotiate with. Say you've got a demanding teenager who begs to use the family car. Since you are concerned about your child's safety (not to mention the condition of the car), your first instinct is to put your foot down and say no. But that will drive a wedge between you and your child and strain your relationship.

This is where skillful negotiation can mean the difference between a harmonious household and a trip to the set of *Family Feud*. You can easily head off an argument with the knowledge you'll gain from this book.

Nothin' Like Friendship

Friendships offer plenty of opportunities for give-and-take. But what do you do when a friend asks for more than you are willing to give?

Let's say that a close friend of yours stops by and asks to borrow a lot of money. She says she needs it to make some urgent repairs on her house. You're sympathetic, but you've also heard that your friend has borrowed from others and hasn't made an effort to pay them back.

What are your choices here? You can hand the money over to your friend and just hope that you get it back. You can bluntly say no and destroy the friendship for good. But once you've read this book, you'll know how to maintain the friendship *without making the loan*. There is a way to do it—if you're savvy about negotiation.

Negotiating on the Job

If you're a salesperson, you know how difficult it can be to impress a potential client— and then close a deal at a profitable price. If you own your own business, you know it's tough to work out terms with your suppliers and customers. But if you're a powerful negotiator, you can work out the best deals for you and your company.

Skillful negotiation can improve even everyday business situations. The next time you're in a committee meeting discussing business strategy, your ideas will be more influential and powerful if you know the best way to present and defend them. If you need a crucial report on a tight deadline, your co-workers will be more likely to oblige if you know how to negotiate with them. When an important customer yells at your boss because a promised order hasn't come in on time, your smooth maneuvering can save the situation—and boost your prestige.

The examples in this chapter are just the tip of the iceberg of challenges you'll face with your families, friends, and co-workers that can be successfully resolved through negotiation. And every time you succeed, your life will be simpler, more profitable, and more enjoyable—I promise.

The Least You Need to Know

➤ You have been negotiating since the moment you were born.

➤ Nearly every facet of your personal and professional life involves negotiation.

➤ Mastering the art of negotiation will help you make more money, perform better on the job, and have better relationships with the people closest to you.

Chapter 2

Scoping Out Your Position

> ### In This Chapter
>
> ➤ Setting your primary and secondary bases
>
> ➤ Preparing concessions
>
> ➤ Developing a plan if no agreement is reached
>
> ➤ Gathering and organizing documents that make your case
>
> ➤ Approaching negotiation with the right attitude

You probably picked up this book for any number of reasons. Maybe you're tired of getting the short end of the stick in your business and personal life. Maybe you just got burned trying to negotiate an important matter such as buying a new home or car. Or maybe you're facing a negotiation that's very important to you: You want to ask your boss for a raise, or you're about to buy a new car, or you want a store manager to replace the defective computer for which you just plunked down $1,000 of your hard-earned money.

Most people aren't naturally good at demanding what they want—that's why classes in assertiveness training are so popular. That's also why the thought of negotiating may make you nervous. How can you get what you want without being a bully? What if you're faced with someone who doesn't want to help you? What if your offer is refused?

As in many other stressful situations, such as giving a speech or throwing a party, a large part of successful negotiation depends on careful preparation and a confident attitude. In this chapter you will learn how to define your position, arm yourself with backup materials, and cloak yourself in confidence.

Prepare Your Position

Just as you wouldn't deliver a speech without thinking about (or writing down) what you plan to say, you can't walk into a negotiation without knowing exactly what you want. It's not enough to think, "It's time I got a raise" or "I'd love to buy that car." Before you settle down to negotiate, you need to define your own position—what you really want, what you're willing to compromise on, and what you can afford to lose.

Your Ideal Deal

Say you've decided to ask for a raise. You can't just storm into the boss's office and demand more money (tempting though that sounds). You'll have to determine your *primary base*: your objective, or your goal. You have to decide your terms in advance: in this case, that means knowing exactly how much you'd like to see in your next paycheck. "I'm currently making $35,000 a year. I'd like a raise of $5,000 to bring my salary up to $40,000."

If you're in the market for a new car, you would first take a realistic look at your budget. After crunching numbers as much as you can, you decide you don't want to spend more than $200 a month for your car payment. That's your primary base.

Realize that the more realistic and reasonable your goal, the more likely you will be to reach it. But how do you decide what a "reasonable" goal is? You have to do some research before you head in to the negotiation. I'll talk more about that in the "Doing Your Homework" section later in this chapter.

To help you start charting your goals, take a look at the following Negotiating Goals worksheet. Many of the issues that frequently crop up in business or personal negotiations are listed on it.

Use the worksheet as a guideline to help you decide which issues will affect your negotiation. You can also rank each item numerically in order of its importance to you.

It's Been Said
"Chance favors the prepared mind."
—Louis Pasteur

Let's Talk Terms
Primary base: the most important issue you negotiate for; your objective; your goal.

Dealmaking Tip
Always set out to win a negotiation by having definite objectives and working to accomplish those objectives.

Negotiating Goals Worksheet

Money: This is probably your biggest issue. How much of a raise do you want? How much would you like to sell your house for? How much will you pay an ad agency to develop a campaign for your widget company?

Your terms: _____

Rank:_____

Payment Schedule: Determining when and how you pay for something is almost as important as how much you pay. Will you get a better deal if you promise cash upfront? Or would you like to spread your payments out over a period of months?

Your terms: _____

Rank:_____

Time: Deadlines can be critical, particularly in business negotiations. How soon do you need to move into a new home? How quickly can the agency get your campaign done? If you are working on a deadline, think about how much you are willing to concede in terms of money in order to get the deal finished on time.

Your terms: _____

Rank:_____

Service: Think of any services you might want after you close the deal if the product or service you are negotiating for proves defective.

Your terms: _____

Rank:_____

Improvements: What kinds of add-ins will you need in the future? This consideration can be important when you buy high-tech items like computers that must be constantly updated with new hardware and software.

Your terms: _____

Rank:_____

Returns: If you are negotiating for a product, how easily can you return it if you're not happy with it? What kind of return (replacement, exchange, or refund) will be available? How much of the original price will you expect to have refunded?

Your terms: _____

Rank:_____

Future Business Tie-Ins: If you close this deal, what kinds of benefits or concessions will you get on future deals?

Your terms: _____

Rank:_____

Volume Deals: Will you earn extra negotiating points if you suggest a large deal? If you're the buyer, can you negotiate for a price break on a larger order? If you're the seller, will you consider giving the buyer a better deal for a larger purchase?

Your terms: _____

Rank:_____

Other: Include any other terms that affect your negotiation here.

Your terms: _____

Rank:_____

Keep in mind that your "ideal deal" may not be the opening offer that you present at the actual negotiation. (I'll talk more about offers in Chapter 21.) Your ideal is simply a yardstick against which you can measure all other offers you receive.

Set Alternative Goals

So you're almost ready to march into your boss's office and ask for a raise. Your clients love you, sales have been soaring since you've come on board, and—most importantly—the company Christmas party you organized last year was a smashing success.

You think you can't lose. But you're caught off-guard when your boss says, "Sure, you deserve a raise. But there's no money in the budget, and there's nothing I can do."

Let's Talk Terms
Alternative goals mean compromises both you and your opponent are willing to make in order to reach a deal.

What should you do? Quit in disgust? Throw a tantrum? Mutter "Maybe next year" and slink away? No way! Well-prepared negotiator that you are, you've decided on some alternative goals you are willing to accept in advance.

Your alternative goals constitute a fallback position—the deal you are willing to settle for if your original suggestion is turned down. So if the boss says no to a raise, follow up with something else: How about more vacation time? More flexible working hours? An agreement to reopen salary negotiations in six months' time? A marble fountain and crushed-velvet carpeting for your cubicle? (Just kidding.)

The beauty of preparing alternative goals in advance is that by arming yourself with alternatives, you can hear the word "no" without losing face. You might even be able to turn a "no" into a "yes."

Look back over the worksheet of negotiables that you filled out earlier. Now use the following table to help you figure out the alternatives for each of the issues that you'll be negotiating.

Ideal Terms	Possible Alternatives

Your Last Resort

Before you negotiate, you should also consider the options you have if you cannot reach an agreement. These options make up your *BATNA*—your *Best Alternative To a Negotiated Agreement*. Developing a BATNA in advance of the negotiation will keep you from accepting poor terms—or turning down terms that you ought to accept.

In the case of asking for a raise, for example, you might say to yourself, "If my boss turns me down, I'll continue working at my job, but I'll approach Company Y and see if that manager position is still open." At this point, that is your BATNA.

Let's Talk Terms
Your *Best Alternative To a Negotiated Agreement (BATNA)* refers to the outcomes or alternatives that remain if no negotiated agreement is reached.

You can always improve your BATNA before you even head into negotiations. Say you interview for the Company Y job *before* you negotiate for your raise. Let's say that Company Y is very impressed with you and makes you a handsome job offer.

That job offer now becomes your new BATNA. You can use it as a yardstick to measure any raise that your current boss offers you. Is your current boss offering you a better deal than Company Y? Or are you undervalued at your present company? That's how BATNA works—as a yardstick to measure any proposal.

Getting on to Second(ary) Bases

Once you've determined what you want, what you're willing to settle for, and what you can afford to lose, you have to consider any and all forces that will work in your favor. Any factors that bolster your primary base are called your *secondary bases*.

Let's talk in terms of that car-buying example. Your primary base was to spend no more than $200 a month for your car payment. Your secondary bases might be that the car salesperson will be working on commission and anxious to make a deal with you, and there are several other dealerships in the area all offering special sales and deals. In other words, it's a buyer's market, and that gives you the negotiating edge.

Let's Talk Terms
Secondary bases are the positive factors that support your primary base. You use them during bargaining to get your primary base.

You may never have to state your secondary bases explicitly once you sit down to the bargaining table. But you should keep them in mind as you negotiate—they will boost your confidence and prevent you from settling for an unsatisfactory deal. Effectively using your secondary bases during the bargaining will get you your primary base.

Doing Your Homework

Once you've ironed out your primary base, secondary bases, and BATNA, it's time to harness all the arguments that support your position. The more hard facts, statistics, and documentation you have, the more difficult it will be for anyone to turn you down.

In simpler negotiations, a quick mental rehearsal of your arguments may be all you need. If you're returning your computer, for example, you should simply gather all the reasons why you think you got a piece of bum equipment. The more specific you can be, the better. ("The mouse freezes up every five minutes, the hard drive spits out my disks, and it deleted the file that contained my great American novel.") The only documentation you'll probably need in this case will be your receipt, the owner's manual, and a copy of the warranty. (You did keep them, didn't you? If you didn't, turn to Chapter 29.)

Dealmaking Tip

As you gather materials to support your case, try to find words or claims that you can use to your advantage. If the owner's manual that comes with your faulty computer frequently praises its dependability, for example, you should underline the word "dependable" every time it appears. Then when you negotiate, keep emphasizing how "dependable" your computer was supposed to be, and how *un*dependable it actually is. You'll give yourself a powerful negotiating advantage.

More complex negotiations (such as bidding for a company, or buying or selling a home), will require more elaborate files and documentation. You don't want to rely on memory alone during the heat of the discussion, when you may be under a lot of pressure. Having all the information you need on paper will also free up your attention to focus on what the other person or people are saying—which is where your concentration *should* be.

Let's say you are about to ask for a raise. You should prepare a file that documents all the backbreaking work you've done. Your file might include:

➤ A list of the successful projects you've spearheaded, the new products rolled out under your supervision, the employees you supervise.

➤ Any favorable financial reports, such as those that show increased sales or profitability, that you can claim responsibility for.

➤ Any letters of praise or recommendation from co-workers or clients.

➤ Comparable salary surveys, if they show that the average salary for your position is substantially higher than what your company is paying you. (One source of this information is the U.S. Department of Labor's Bureau of Labor Statistics.)

Get Organized

All the files in the world won't help you if they're spilling out of your briefcase onto the floor. You don't want to break a deep discussion while you fumble for a document or search for an important piece of information. If you aren't organized, you will appear less effective and less competent and you could lose your negotiating momentum.

When I walk up to a negotiating table, I like to have the documents related to each major subject under negotiation separated into individual folders. I label each folder with a large, boldly written title that's easy to read. I sometimes use different-colored inks to help me locate specific paragraphs or ideas in a file.

Here is an example of an organizational system you might use, with different-colored folders, when you're negotiating to buy your dream home:

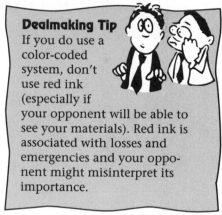

Dealmaking Tip
If you have more than one issue to negotiate— for example, both the price of a car and the options it comes with—spend the bulk of your organizing time on the largest, most important issue.

Dealmaking Tip
If you do use a color-coded system, don't use red ink (especially if your opponent will be able to see your materials). Red ink is associated with losses and emergencies and your opponent might misinterpret its importance.

Financial

This file contains information on all matters financial, including the offering price, real-estate taxes, and sewer, water, or street levies. It should also include any add-ons that may raise the price of the home, such as appliances.

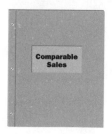

Comparable Sales

This file contains sales data on similar homes (especially those in the immediate area of the home you want to buy). During the negotiation, you'll want to call special attention to comparable homes whose sales prices are lower than your seller's offering price.

This file contains any and all written offers or counteroffers made by you or the seller. It should also include all correspondence relevant to the transaction, placed in chronological order.

This file contains all matters relevant to title, including title insurance and any title defects (such as a neighbor's tree that encroaches on the property) that must be cleared by the seller before a title can pass to you if you purchase the property.

This file contains information on all the conditions that must be met before the deal can be finalized: financing, house inspection, surveying the property, and so on.

Dealbreaker Alert

Once you're into a negotiation, never leave your files unattended, especially during short breaks. They'll be too vulnerable to prying eyes. Always take them with you.

If you decide to bring pictures or other graphic data, keep them in a separate file. Do the same with physical exhibits such as posters, titles, and deeds. You don't want them to detract from your presentation until you are actually ready to use them. (In Chapter 6 you'll learn more about using props in negotiation.)

Who Else Is on Your Side?

In most of the everyday negotiations I discuss in this book, you can successfully and confidently represent yourself. But certain negotiations that carry important financial or legal ramifications (such as buying or selling a home or negotiating a labor issue) require professional help. In those cases, you might consider hiring one of the following:

> ➤ *Lawyer.* A lawyer is an individual who is knowledgeable about the law and licensed to assist people with their legal needs. Some lawyers have general practices and deal with a variety of legal issues; others limit their practices to particular areas (real-estate law, personal injury law, divorce law, and so on).

> ➤ *Broker or agent.* You may use a broker or agent when you buy or sell a home or real estate (see Part 7).

> ➤ *Mediator.* If you can't reach an agreement with your opponent, you might call in a mediator. See Chapter 20 for more information about mediators.

> ➤ *Arbitrator.* An arbitrator is another party who can settle a dispute. See Chapter 20 for more information about arbitrators.

Dealmaking Tip
How do you find a good lawyer? First ask your friends and acquaintances for referrals. You can also check the yellow pages, or ask your local bar association for a membership directory. Many lawyers offer free consultations, in which you can discuss your case and decide if you'd like to hire the lawyer to represent you.

Be aware that the responsibilities and definitions of lawyers, brokers, agents, mediators, and arbitrators differ from state to state. If you consider hiring one of these experts, be sure to consult your local attorney or bar association to find out the rules and regulations in your state.

Psyche Yourself Up for Negotiation

So now you know your terms and you're loaded down with files and documents that bolster your case. There's one last crucial piece of ammunition that you need: confidence.

Before you can be successful in any negotiation, you must *believe* that you can be successful. Once you've settled your position, review the issue from all angles until you're fully convinced of the merits of your case. Your conviction and enthusiasm will be obvious when you negotiate.

It's Been Said
"The world of achievement has always belonged to the optimist."
—J. Harold Wilkins

One of the best ways to develop a positive mental attitude is to practice it every day, in everything you do. You can't expect to radiate optimism and competence during negotiation if you walk around feeling pessimistic and hopeless about everything else that happens in your life.

So try to maintain a positive mental attitude on small matters as well as large. (Not only will you be a better negotiator, but you'll be more fun to be around!) Believe that you can change a tire, win a game of tennis, bake a mouth-watering loaf of bread, snatch the last available seat on the subway, conquer whatever challenges you face. That belief will foster the positive attitude that will help you win virtually any negotiation, large or small, simple or complex.

The Least You Need to Know

➤ Define your goals and alternative goals before you enter into any negotiation.

➤ Use your BATNA—Best Alternative To a Negotiated Agreement—as a guideline to evaluate all proposals and agreements.

➤ Prepare and organize all materials that will back up your position before you enter into negotiation.

➤ A positive mental attitude will boost your powers of persuasion and make you a better negotiator.

AND THE BIG
GUY IS GETTING
INTO A HONDA.
BLUE WITH RED INTERIOR.

Chapter 3

What's the Other Side Up To?

In This Chapter

➤ Identifying your opponent

➤ Understanding your opponent's position

➤ Preparing to equalize your opponent's position

➤ Turning your opponent into your ally

Although it may sound hostile, I'm using the term *opponent* throughout this book to distinguish between the opposing sides in any negotiation. No matter what type of negotiation you enter into, you will face another side or opponent.

Obviously, in many situations that opponent will be a friend, colleague, or family member—someone whom you like and whose company you enjoy. So the use of the term "opponent" here is not meant to suggest that you have an antagonistic relationship with the person you negotiate with.

Other negotiating books use phrases like "the other side" or "the person you are negotiating with" to distinguish between negotiating sides. I decided against those phrases only because opponent seemed easier to understand and more to the point.

This chapter teaches you how to understand and predict your opponent's moves—before you reach the negotiating table.

Take Me to Your Leader

Before you begin negotiating, you need to figure out who has the authority to make all final decisions involving the negotiation. That's the person who can say "yes" to you. In fact, let's call that person the "yes" person. If you don't deal with the "yes" person, negotiation will be difficult (or even impossible) for a number of reasons:

➤ You won't be displaying your finely honed negotiating skills to the person who most needs to see them.

➤ You won't be able to observe and influence the "yes" person during the hottest point of the negotiations. The "yes" person will be safely insulated from any argument or debate that arises.

➤ Your position might not be correctly relayed to the "yes" person.

Let's Talk Terms
The *"yes" person*: the person who has the authority to resolve the issue you are trying to negotiate.

It's usually fairly easy to identify the "yes" person. If you're interested in buying something (a house, a car, a tea set), you can safely assume that the owner of the item is the "yes" person. If you're negotiating with a small business, you will generally negotiate with the store manager or company owner.

Dealbreaker Alert

Lawyers are not obligated to have their clients present during negotiations. If your opponent has a lawyer, you might be stuck dealing with the lawyer rather than the "yes" person (the client). Ask if the lawyer will bring her client to the bargaining table anyway. An inexperienced lawyer might agree—which gives you an excellent chance to influence the "yes" person directly.

In other situations (for example, if you're dealing with a large corporation with a complex hierarchy), the "yes" person might not be immediately obvious. If you're in doubt, ask who has the authority to resolve the matter. Then arrange to meet with that person.

On occasion, the "yes" person might not be a decisive individual, but one who prefers to think matters over or consult with others. Don't object to that. You don't want to push too hard and risk turning the "yes" person off.

On other occasions, you might bargain with someone who is not the "yes" person but who still acts decisively, as if he can agree to a deal. If that person is an agent of the "yes" person and is acting within the scope of his authority, then don't hesitate to close the deal. When you do, however, you run some risk because the person you are dealing with may *not* have the authority to bind the "yes" person to a deal.

In the final analysis, then, try to bargain with the "yes" person whenever possible. It's the surest way to get results.

If the "Yes" Person Doesn't Show (or Brings Friends)

As you plan your negotiating strategy, always direct your argument to the "yes" person—even if there will be other people present, or if the "yes" person is not present. You want to be tactful and subtle when you do this, because you want to treat everyone with whom you bargain with respect and courtesy. The "yes" person's colleagues will undoubtedly tell her about your behavior and advise her whether or not to deal with you.

Dealbreaker Alert

If you know you will be dealing with someone other than the "yes" person, you will have to be especially sure to keep your speech short and simple. The more complicated your arguments, the greater the chance that they will not be accurately passed along to the "yes" person.

Say you bought a new boat, which promptly started to sink every time you tried to sail. Each time, the dealer sent a repair person to fix your boat's problems. But when the engine finally spluttered out and almost moored you on the high seas, you decided to ask for your money back.

The dealer's employees tell you they don't want to give you a refund—instead, they offer to continue to repair the defects, or get you another boat. You advise the employees that you want to deal with the owner of the dealership—the "yes" person. He is the one who has the most to gain or lose if you are a happy or dissatisfied customer.

The owner avoids you (not surprising, considering the quality of his product) and you find that you must instead talk to his employees. You should still direct the brunt of what you're saying toward the owner. Mention how much you would like to continue to do business with the owner, or any other legitimate issue that will influence the owner directly. This is the way to ensure smooth negotiating sailing. (Sorry about the pun. I couldn't help myself!)

Researching Your Opponent

The more you can learn about your opponent before you negotiate, the more effective and successful you'll be at the bargaining table. Depending on the type of negotiating you'll be doing, you should check out some of the following sources of information:

➤ *Ask others in the business.* Most people know a lot about their colleagues and competitors. For example, if you're about to negotiate with a mechanic who botched your car repair, you could ask other mechanics for more information on what kind of repair needed to be done, how your mechanic operates, and so on. Business people routinely do this type of checking.

➤ *Check with your local library.* This is a fertile source of information. You can check *Who's Who* directories, business listings, and the *Encyclopedia of Associations* (see next point) for information. Ask your librarian for help.

➤ *Check with associations.* The *Encyclopedia of Associations* will give you a listing of all the trade associations your opponent may belong to (for example, the Bar Association, real estate associations, medical associations, and many more). Many trade organizations provide biographies and directories of their members. These materials can be a good source of information.

➤ *Check with a stockbroker.* If you are involved in a business negotiation, a stockbroker can get you a wealth of information (annual reports, changes in executive personnel, and so on) on any company whose stock is publicly traded.

Let's say you're being wooed by a company for a sales position. You've researched the company thoroughly by scouring its annual reports, reading industry newsletters, and talking to friends in the business. You find that the company is getting trounced by its chief competitor and that earnings have decreased over the last three years.

Dealmaking Tip

Try to learn as much about your opponent as you can before you begin negotiating. That'll give you a much greater chance of finding common ground, developing a rapport, and influencing your opponent to agree to a deal.

Now when you sit down to discuss the position, you've got the upper hand. You know your new job will be difficult (and possibly short-lived, if the company's finances don't improve). So you can bargain for a better salary and benefits package.

Making Your Opponent Happy

You should also try to figure out what your opponent's goals and motivators are. (Anything that influences someone to act is a *motivator*.) If you can find something in your proposal that is attractive or beneficial to the person you're negotiating with, you'll have a much better chance of conducting a successful negotiation.

For example, most salespeople work on a straight commission (the money they earn is based on the sales they make, rather than a fixed salary or hourly wage). If you're in the market to buy something, you can aim for a bargain while the salesperson aims to make a sale. Then you'll both be happy.

Dealmaking Tip

Your opponent wants to feel good about any agreement reached with you. So always point out any benefits that your proposal offers to your opponent.

Or say you're eyeing a new home and the broker reveals that the seller is anxious to make a quick sale because she's transferring to a new job. Now you can assume that the seller will accept any reasonable offer you make.

The following worksheet helps you identify the goals of both parties. For every one of your goals, think of what your opponent will want—then brainstorm a compromise that lets you both get what you want.

Your Goals	Your Opponent's Goals	Terms That Satisfy Both Sides
_____	_____	_____
_____	_____	_____
_____	_____	_____
_____	_____	_____
_____	_____	_____
_____	_____	_____

> **Dealmaking Tip**
>
> When it comes to selling a home, brokers are prone to giving away information about the seller because they want to make the sale. If you are negotiating with a broker, find out as much as you can about the seller's situation. If a broker is representing you, be careful not to give him information that you don't want a potential buyer to hear.

What If You Both Can't Win?

Unfortunately, in certain negotiations there's just no way to have both parties walk away from the bargaining table feeling good about the outcome. This is especially true for negotiations that involve settling disputes. In fact, a majority of court cases that involve disputes stem from negotiations that could not be settled at the bargaining table.

What's your approach when it's obvious that your opponent is not going to feel good about the outcome? Strive to accomplish your negotiating objectives. Don't cave in on your bargaining goals just to make your opponent feel good about the outcome. That may seem harsh, but it's not. Your opponent has the same goal—to accomplish her bargaining objectives.

Anticipating Your Opponent's Moves

Once you've established your opponent's motives, you'll be able to predict how he will act at the bargaining table. When you know in advance what arguments he will raise, you'll be able to answer each one of them.

Equalization is the ability to answer your opponent's positions or arguments with equally compelling positions of your own. Equalization is absolutely essential. If your opponent raises an issue that you can't equalize, his argument will remain hanging in the air with no response. Then you'll never convince him to meet your terms.

One way you can anticipate and understand your opponent's moves is to think about what *you* will do at the bargaining table. Whatever arguments you plan to use, assume that he will be thinking along the same lines—only from the opposite side.

For example, say you're preparing to buy a new home. The one you're interested in is in a great location, and it has a lot of potential, but there are also quite a few flaws with the place. The sellers, Joe and Jane Jones, are asking for a lot more money than you are willing to pay. You want the place, but only at a better price.

One of your strategies is to point out the defects in the property—the leaky roof, the old siding, the cracks in the driveway, the ancient wheezing furnace. Then you think: How will the Joneses counteract my arguments? By pointing out all the pluses of their house, and possibly by soft-pedaling the defects.

Four Ways to Equalize Your Opponent's Position

Here are four good ways you can equalize your opponent's positions:

➤ *Show that your opponent's position is not well founded.* Say you think the Joneses will point out the house's virtues—the new avocado living-room carpet, the lush lawn, and the large backyard shed. If you can prove that these wonders do not offset the costs of the roof, the siding, the driveway, and the furnace, then you've disproved their position.

➤ *Distinguish your opponent's position.* Say the Joneses claim that similar houses in the neighborhood sell for the same price that they are asking. You check around and learn that the other homes are substantially newer and better maintained. Then you are prepared to distinguish the Joneses' home with the others.

➤ *Advance your own position, which is equal to or greater than your opponent's position.* You did this when you asserted that the repair work you will have to put into the house (fix the roof, the siding, the driveway, and the furnace) more than equals the worth of the work the Joneses have already done.

➤ *Show that your opponent's position is not relevant or material.* The Joneses tell you that they have a close friend who thinks their asking price is actually too low. Unless their friend is in the real estate business, though, her opinion isn't really relevant to your negotiation. You can point that out to equalize the Joneses' position.

One more word about equalization. Realize that sometimes when you negotiate, your opponent will hit you with bizarre, even laughable positions. But you have to equalize each and every position your opponent puts forward. If you don't, your opponent will still believe in it, and use it as a barrier to giving you what you want.

Equalization in Action

To give you an example of a well-prepared negotiation strategy, say you have to prepare a report for your boss by early next week. You need some figures from Monica, a colleague of yours in the marketing department. But Monica says she's swamped and won't have time to run the numbers till next Thursday, at the earliest. What can you do?

You have to equalize Monica's assertion that "she's swamped." You can do this in a variety of ways: by showing her that the information you need won't take a lot of time to prepare; or by offering to help her with it; or by offering to take some other project or chore off her hands. Or you can advance your own position by emphasizing how important this project is to your boss, and how much credit both you and Monica will reap if the project is well received. Any of these suggestions should be enough to equalize Monica's position.

Your Equalization Worksheet

Fill in the following worksheet as you prepare your arguments and counterarguments. By preparing some key points in advance, you'll be much more eloquent—and persuasive—when you reach the actual negotiation.

Your Argument	Your Opponent's Argument	Your Counter-Argument
_____	_____	_____
_____	_____	_____
_____	_____	_____
_____	_____	_____
_____	_____	_____
_____	_____	_____

The Least You Need to Know

➤ Before you begin negotiating, you have to identify the "yes" person—the person who has the power to give you what you want.

➤ All your arguments should be targeted toward the "yes" person, whether or not that person will actually be present during the negotiation.

➤ Find out as much information as you can about your opponent before you reach the bargaining table.

➤ You will have the best chance of succeeding if you can meet at least some of your opponent's goals.

➤ As you prepare for negotiation, examine your moves to discover your opponent's countermoves.

➤ You must equalize every position your opponent advances, even if you consider a position ridiculous.

Chapter 4

Get Ready, Get Set...Negotiate!

In This Chapter

➤ Arranging the best place and time for negotiation

➤ How to look and act when you negotiate

➤ What to do if you are caught off-guard by a negotiation

➤ How to open a negotiation

➤ How to rescue a negotiation that gets off to a bad start

I once had a client who liked to swing all of his big business deals in his office conference room during his lunch hour. His negotiations were sumptuous affairs, with catering provided by a swank nearby hotel. His opponents were dazzled by the colorful trays of food laid out on the conference room table. They feasted on platefuls of food, while he only nibbled.

My client wasn't just being a generous, hospitable guy. Controlling the place and time of his meetings was one way that he secured his hold over the negotiations. Lulling his opponents with rich food—while he himself did not indulge—was another way he maintained his mental edge.

In this chapter, you learn how to arrange and open negotiations so that you maintain the negotiating edge.

Setting the Stage

Once you've worked through the previous chapters and planned your arguments and counterarguments, you're ready to begin negotiating. All you need to do is arrange a meeting. But wait! There are subtle nuances of time and place that can work for you— or against you—before you even open your mouth to begin negotiating. Read on.

Stay on Home Turf

Ask any sports team where they'd prefer to play the big game and without exception they'll say on their home field. That's the place where they are most comfortable and where they won't have to deal with unfamiliar territory. That's also where their opponents are the most uncomfortable.

That's where you want to play the negotiating game—on your *home field*. Your home field is any place that you are familiar with and where you feel completely comfortable. Depending on the negotiation, you might use your office, home, car, or even a restaurant or club that you visit regularly as your home field.

Why is negotiating on home base so important? When you negotiate on home field, your concentration won't be broken by trying to adjust to unfamiliar (and possibly uncomfortable) surroundings—but your opponent's will. That gives you the edge.

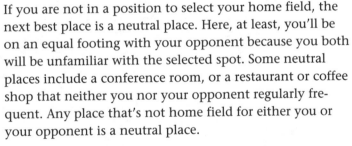

If you are not in a position to select your home field, the next best place is a neutral place. Here, at least, you'll be on an equal footing with your opponent because you both will be unfamiliar with the selected spot. Some neutral places include a conference room, or a restaurant or coffee shop that neither you nor your opponent regularly frequent. Any place that's not home field for either you or your opponent is a neutral place.

The last place you want to negotiate? You guessed it. Avoid your opponent's home field like the plague.

In some negotiations, this is easier said than done. When you buy a new car, for example, your early negotiations will take place at the dealer's showroom—your opponent's home field. It's unavoidable. However, there are steps you can take to help neutralize the situation.

Don't go into the salesperson's office to discuss the deal. Try to avoid the showroom, too—it's still pretty much the territory of the salesperson. If it's a nice day, walk outside

Dealmaking Tip
One of the earliest tip-offs that your opponent is not a skilled negotiator is if he asks where you want to meet to discuss the matter. No experienced negotiator will!

Dealmaking Tip
Never hesitate to let your opponent know where you want to negotiate. In most cases, you'll get your way.

and discuss the deal there. Now you're luring the salesperson away from his turf. And even if you are stuck on the lot for the early discussions, you can reclaim your advantage by changing the site of the closing. (In Chapter 22 you will learn more about the art of closing the deal.)

There will be occasions when you'll get trapped into negotiating on your opponent's home field. Your boss, for example, might collar you in the hallway and ask you to come back to her office to discuss an important project she wants you to take on (one that you have no extra time for). What do you do then?

➤ Try to move the negotiation to your home field, if you can, by suggesting that you have to get some papers or materials from your desk.

➤ If you can't get away from your opponent's home field, try to assert yourself by standing up, or moving around, rather than sitting.

➤ Don't be the first person to speak. Let your opponent open the negotiation so you have an extra chance to understand what her position is—and decide what your own approach should be.

Dealbreaker Alert

One of the biggest mistakes people make when they're after a raise or promotion is to pop the question in the boss's office. That's where your boss is most comfortable and the most difficult to persuade. If at all possible, try to lure your boss into your office. (Not only will you be on home turf, but your massive files and humming computer will prove your productivity.) If that isn't possible, try for a neutral conference room or nearby restaurant.

Timing Is Everything

It's important that you negotiate when you are at your physical peak. So whenever possible, choose the time that works best with your own personal make-up.

Each of us has a metabolism that, together with our personal traits and habits, governs our actions. If you're a late riser and don't get rolling until after lunch, try to do all of your negotiating later in the day. On the other hand, if you're alert the moment you open your eyes in the morning, do your negotiating then.

Remember my client who lulled his opponents into a stupor with food? Eating a heavy meal will dull your mind and slow your responses. So eat lightly before you negotiate—

just enough to keep you mentally alert, no more. Avoid alcoholic beverages. If you overindulge before a negotiation, you're penalizing yourself and giving the edge to your opponent.

What Should You Wear?

If you had a serious problem and you walked into a lawyer's office to get some help, you'd be shocked if the lawyer wore rumpled, smelly clothes and badly needed a haircut. (Unless the lawyer was Columbo.)

In negotiation (as in almost everything else), you will be judged by how you look. And the first impression you create is the most lasting one. If you look competent and professional, your opponent is more likely to believe that you are.

It's Been Said
"The world is governed more by appearance than by realities."
—Daniel Webster

Dealmaking Tip
A number of books and articles have been written about how to "power dress" when you negotiate—for example, wearing the powerful color red when you charge in to ask your boss for a raise. During my long negotiating career, I've been confronted with every kind of dress and color scheme, and my opponent's wardrobe has never had any kind of effect on me.

Your objective is to get your opponent to focus on what you're saying and doing—not on what you're wearing. The key is to be natural. Wear clothes that you are comfortable in. Wear conservative colors such as browns, blues, and grays, and avoid flashy styles and clunky accessories. They'll focus your attention on what you're wearing—not on what you're saying or doing.

How you dress has one other important impact. It affects not only how well your opponent hears your argument, but also how your opponent sees you as a person. If you dress in expensive Armani, for example, your opponent will see you as a person with deep pockets—not the image you want to project if you are hunting for a bargain. Make sure your clothing projects an image appropriate to your negotiation.

Help! I'm Not Ready for This!

What if someone approaches you with a negotiation, and you simply aren't ready? Basically, you'll have to devise some kind of stalling tactic. You can try to postpone, if you have a more pressing meeting or project on your hands. Or you can simply admit, "I really want to discuss this with you, but I haven't had a chance to think about it yet." Then set up a meeting for a later date.

Your Opening Moves

How you start a negotiation will have an important—even crucial—impact on its final outcome. As the saying goes, "You never get a second chance to make a good first impression." A good first impression makes your opponent more receptive to your entire presentation—and may take you one step closer to getting what you want. Making the right opening moves sets the tone for the remainder of your negotiating game.

You want to win the respect of your opponent as early as possible—and that won't happen if you're flustered, haggard, or unforgivably late. Make sure you've got precise instructions as to where and when the meeting will happen—then make it a point to get there early.

Never start a negotiation until you are comfortably settled. Stash your coat, purse, and any other items you won't need during the negotiation. Take a minute to flip through your materials, if you have any, and make sure everything is in order. Review any notes you've made that you think you might use during the bargaining.

Even if you can't function without coffee (I know the feeling), you should toss any cups before you sit down. You don't want a container to shield you from your opponent just at the point when you want to make an impression. (You also don't want to risk scalding yourself in the middle of the meeting.) Get a refill after the discussions have started and after you've already made your first impression.

It's Been Said
"Well begun is half done."   —Aristotle

Setting the Mood

When you meet your opponent for the first time, do so with a warm, genuine smile—even if you're nervous about the upcoming negotiation. A smile says that you are prepared to approach the negotiation on an objective basis, even if it might turn difficult or controversial. Your smile is also a sign of confidence.

Once you've smiled and introduced yourself to your opponent (if he is a new one), you want to find some kind of common ground. This not only helps break the ice, but also convinces your opponent that you are a capable person.

Many people are uneasy making small talk, but it isn't difficult. There are a variety of approaches you can take, and any one will do, as long as you remember one thing: be genuine. You don't want to appear insincere at this crucial stage, when you're trying to make a good first impression.

If you took my advice back in Chapter 3 and researched your opponent, you should already know a little bit about his work experiences or personal interests. If you're familiar with your opponent's work, for example, you might want to talk about the projects he's handling or the state of the industry. If you've negotiated similar matters before, don't be reluctant to (tactfully) point this out as well ("I've handled deals with several other store accounts, and they've all been happy with Acme Widgets. I'm sure you and I will work well together too.").

Other reliable small-talk subjects include:

➤ Weather. Sure, it's a cliché, but it can form a springboard to many other subjects ("It's so beautiful outside. Perfect weather for sailing." "Isn't this rain awful? I feel like holing up at home with this great new book I've got.").

➤ Common hobbies, like camping, gardening, sports, cooking, reading, music, and so on. Stay alert and look for cues as to what hobbies your opponent is interested in.

➤ Travel and places you've both visited.

➤ The trials and tribulations of raising kids (if both you and your opponent have them) or pets (ditto).

Do whatever you can to put your opponent in a positive frame of mind before you get into the brunt of your case. If you show up at your local auto dealer to complain about the lemon you've bought, don't launch into a litany of complaints. You might start off by saying instead that you and your family are good customers of the dealership. That flatters your opponent, breaks the ice, and makes the dealer anxious not to alienate you—he could lose many customers if he doesn't treat you right.

Dealbreaker Alert

If you rush into business too quickly, before you cultivate a positive negotiating environment, your opponent may become defensive and resist giving you what you want—even if your position is a solid one.

If you're talking with your boss about a raise, you can set an upbeat mood by first mentioning your latest office success, or an important project you've recently completed ("Here are the monthly sales figures on the new line of widgets. They've been flying out of the stores."). Now you've got your boss in the proper frame of mind and have paved your way into the next phase—dazzling your boss with your excellent track record and capping that off with your request for a raise.

Taking the Plunge

When you've finished with the small talk, you should explain why you're there. Be concise and polite. Don't say, "The car is a piece of trash." Say, "I'm disappointed in the car I bought here," and then list specifically what's going wrong with it.

You want to start mild so you can test your opponent's reaction. If your opponent doesn't seem particularly concerned or upset, that's a good sign that he's in a receptive mood.

But maybe things don't go so smoothly. Perhaps when you start to state your case, your opponent winces or reacts with disbelief. You should acknowledge his reaction and ask why he's reacting that way. Maybe it has nothing to do with you—he's just having a bad day and his problems are affecting your meeting. If that's the case, ask if he wants to reschedule. Better to postpone negotiations than to deal with an opponent who is in a bad mood at the outset.

But what if *you* are the cause of your opponent's mood? What if he says, "There's nothing wrong with my cars. Maybe if you weren't such a lousy driver you wouldn't have so many problems."

I'll talk more about keeping emotions out of negotiation in Part 5. For now, you've got to tactfully convince your opponent that his bad attitude is unjustified. You want to coax him back into a receptive mood—not convince him of the merits of your position.

In the auto dealer's case, no one likes to be confronted with his own poor workmanship or defective products. You might try to clear the air by simply pointing out that the discussion is not pleasant for either of you, that you would like to continue to shop at his dealership, and that you know you both want to work out a "fair and reasonable" solution. The words *"fair and reasonable"* usually work like magic. Everyone wants to believe that they are fair and reasonable people! So repeatedly suggest that you are looking for a "fair and reasonable" solution.

By suggesting that you both have the same goals—a desire to be fair, to solve the problem, and to maintain a business relationship—you make it seem as though both of you are on the same side. Usually, this approach will calm down your opponent. (It will also boost your confidence in your negotiating powers.)

Once you've established a genial mood and common ground, plunge into the substance of your position. Refer to your documentation (if you've brought any). Be bold.

> **Dealmaking Tip**
> Getting your opponent to say "yes" should be one of your early objectives—you want to form a bond between the two of you, and you want to set an agreeable, friendly mood. One way to do this is to discuss a common interest, concern, or viewpoint that you and your opponent both share.

What if I'm Rebuffed?

Very few people will turn you away if you open negotiations in a friendly, professional manner. Still, on occasion you may run into an opponent who refuses to deal with you. (For example, a salesperson who says, "Sorry—absolutely no refunds, ever.") What do you do if you are snubbed?

Dealmaking Tip
If your opponent makes an obviously valid point, acknowledge it. That will promote progress and actually work to your advantage. By arguing your opponent's valid points, you will make him less receptive to anything you say or do.

➤ Stay pleasant and smile—it's disarming.

➤ Immediately come back with a reasonable response. Say, for example, that it would be in the best interests of both of you to settle the issue in a professional, cordial manner.

➤ Don't get angry. (I discuss the problem of anger in negotiation in Chapter 18.)

➤ If all else fails, don't quit. Tell your opponent you'll come back to discuss the issue at a later time. (Set an actual time, if possible.) That gives your opponent time to cool off; it also gives you time to plan a new strategy.

The Least You Need to Know

➤ Always try to negotiate on your home field—the place you are most comfortable.

➤ Choose the time of day when you're at your mental peak to negotiate.

➤ Wear comfortable clothes when negotiating. Choose your clothes to suit the situation.

➤ If you are caught off-guard by a negotiation, reschedule it for a better time.

➤ Try to establish your credibility and discover common ground with your opponent before you launch into your bargaining position.

➤ Open negotiations with confidence. If your opponent seems reluctant to deal with you, suggest that you both have a common interest in resolving the issue.

Part 2
At the Bargaining Table: Basic Negotiating Techniques

Any art that is worth mastering is built on small techniques. There are cooking techniques, gardening techniques, driving techniques, and even breathing techniques.

There are also negotiating techniques. They're your method or means of carrying out your plan of action. Their purpose is to motivate your opponent to reach an agreement with you.

When your negotiating bag of tricks contains a variety of bargaining techniques, you're equipped with many different ways to reach your goal. You can pick and choose the right technique to get the best results. In this part, I take you through the basic techniques that you need to negotiate successfully.

Chapter 5

Word Power: The Language of Negotiation

In This Chapter

➤ The importance of simple language

➤ Using descriptive language

➤ Speaking your opponent's language

➤ The impact of silence

➤ Boosting your power of communication

I once negotiated the purchase of a large building, for which the seller wanted over a million dollars. I raised the issue of the high costs of replacing the plumbing and electrical wiring. My opponent said the wiring problem was "curable functional obsolescence." Huh? Couldn't he just say that the outdated wiring could be replaced?

Words, wrote Rudyard Kipling, are "the most powerful drug used by mankind." The words you use are the most powerful tools in your negotiating arsenal. In this chapter, you learn how and when to use the right words.

Keep It Simple

At all stages of negotiation, it's important to speak clearly so there is no danger of misinterpretation. Avoid strange words or general, catch-all phrases, which may not convey the message you are trying to send and will often call for additional explanations. The following table shows some examples of what I mean.

Hard to Understand	Easier to Understand
Execution of documents	Signing the papers
Renumeration	Salary; wages; any financial benefit
To wit	Namely
Tendering possession	Moving out
Warrants	Promises

Try to avoid words, terms, or phrases that have multiple meanings. If they must be used, be sure to define them early in the negotiation to avoid any later misunderstandings.

Use Descriptive Language

Here's a true story that clearly illustrates the power of descriptive language. A lawyer represented a boy who had lost both arms in a train accident. When the lawyer made his final argument to the jury, he simply said, "Ladies and gentlemen, I just had lunch with this boy. He eats just like a dog." His image was attention-grabbing language at its finest. The jury ruled for the injured boy.

That's precisely what you want language to do—get your opponent's attention. Before you negotiate, think about the most persuasive words and phrases you can use to give your presentation impact. Remember that your words are the vehicles that drive thoughts from your mind to your opponent's mind. Would you rather send your thoughts in a Lexus or a car ready for the junk heap?

It's Been Said
"To get your ideas across, use small words, big ideas, and short sentences."
—J.H. Patterson

Use concrete details to describe a situation, rather than a general statement. The more you can bring the matter alive with vivid mental pictures, the more persuasive you will be.

Avoid catch-all phrases—they're too broad to have any meaningful impact. Don't close a negotiation by saying, "That takes in the whole ball of wax." You'd be better off saying: "So now we're in agreement on the sales price, the quantity, the shipping date, and the terms of payment." The following table shows some more examples of phrases to avoid.

Catch-All Phrase	Specific Terms
"We've settled everything." (commonly used when closing a bargaining session)	"We've settled the following points: (list specific terms)."
"Financial package." (commonly used in business negotiations and salary discussions)	"We've agreed upon these finances: (list specific terms)."
"Settlement package."	"The settlement terms are as follows: (list specific terms)."
"Under warranty."	"The warranty for (list specific product) includes (list specific terms of warranty)."
"Repair job" or "Remodel job."	"(Mention specific product) will have (list specific problem) repaired for (list agreed-upon price)."

Negotiating Hall of Fame

Two priests were so addicted to smoking that they desperately needed to puff on cigarettes even while they prayed. Both developed guilty consciences and decided to ask their superior for permission to smoke.

The first asked if it was okay to smoke while he was praying. Permission was denied. The second priest asked if he was allowed to pray while he was smoking. His superior found his dedication admirable and immediately granted his request.

Say you're selling your car and you want to emphasize how well it's been maintained. You can say that the car is in very good condition—or you can relate all the tune-ups, oil changes, and washing and waxing you've done. Your detailed description (supported, if possible, with receipts) will make a much greater impact on your opponent.

Speak Your Opponent's Language

Every profession has its own specialized language, or *jargon*. If you're going to be negotiating a deal that involves technical knowledge—such as a complex real estate deal or a complicated car repair—you'll need to be familiar with the lingo.

The following table shows some examples of jargon you may encounter in particular negotiating situations.

Buying a Home	Leasing a Car	Appraising Property
Warranty deed	Closed lease	Appraiser
Lien	Lessor	Fair market value
Escrow	Lessee	Highest and best use
Fixtures	Leasing agreement	Depreciation
Special assessments	Security deposit	Cost approach
Survey	Trade-in allowance	Income capitalization approach
Mortgage	Standards for wear and use	Comparable sales approach
Mortgagor	Wholesale value at end of lease	
Mortgagee		
Title policy		

Speaking your opponent's language boosts your negotiating power for a number of reasons:

➤ Your opponent will immediately understand and relate to what you're saying.

➤ Your opponent will be much more likely to be influenced by what you're saying.

➤ Your opponent will recognize you as an equal.

Let's Talk Terms
Jargon is the specialized language of a particular organization, occupation, or group.

Think about all the ads for car leasing you've seen these days—they're hotbeds of jargon and specialized terminology. If you're in the market to lease a car, the agent might mention a "closed lease." At the outset, you'd want the leasing agent to define the term. (For the record, it means that at the end of the lease you can return the car with no further obligations.)

Or, if you work in real estate, you understand the difference between a "net lease," a "net, net lease," or even a "net, net, net lease." (Imagine how confusing it must be to use them in conversation—they even look puzzling on paper!)

So make it clear at the outset that when you say "net, net, net lease," you are talking about a lease in which the tenant pays all taxes, insurance, repairs, and maintenance, and other charges and expenses of operating and maintaining the property, and the rent the property owner receives is free of all those charges and expenses.

Dealmaking Tip
If you don't understand the words or phrases your opponent uses, ask for an explanation. It's not a sign of weakness—it's good negotiating.

If your opponent is using language you don't understand, don't hesitate to ask her to repeat or clarify a statement.

Once you know what the term means and are comfortable with it, you can freely use it during the discussions in order to communicate more effectively with your opponent.

The Sound of Silence

Silence, as Winston Churchill once observed, "enhances one's authority." Don't assume that you have to out-talk your opponent to win at negotiation. You have too much to lose by mouthing off indiscriminately:

➤ You lose the opportunity to think about what you should be saying and when you should be saying it.

➤ You lose the chance to hear your opponent's positions and formulate the best response to them.

➤ You may inadvertently blurt out information that damages your negotiating position.

If you're in doubt as to whether to speak—or what you want to say—the best approach is to remain silent. If you reveal or blurt out information harmful to your position, you've made yourself fair game for your opponent.

I once represented a widow whose husband's poorly drafted will caused her a great deal of financial confusion. Her tax statements were audited, and the revenue agent who reviewed the case started claiming that she owed a lot of money. I tried to convince him that she didn't, but he wouldn't let up.

After several arduous conversations, he finally blurted out the real reason he was pursuing her so doggedly: she was a "test case." The government sometimes tries these cases in order to set future tax policy. My client, in other words, was being used as sort of a legal guinea pig. Once I knew that, I figured out how to remove her situation from the "test case" category, and the issue was settled.

Use silence strategically after you've made a solid point. This gives your opponent time to fully absorb your meaning and encourages him to draw his own conclusions. Since we're all powerfully influenced by our own conclusions—rather than what someone else tells us to believe—silence is a powerful negotiating tool.

Remain silent after your opponent has made a proposal— your silence suggests disappointment or disapproval. Your opponent may rush in, offering concessions that will sweeten the deal. Whenever an opponent makes a proposal—whether it's a good one or not—always consider giving it the silent treatment.

What if you're a constant chatterbox who finds it difficult to remain silent? If you are uncomfortable with silence (many people are), there are some easy techniques you can use to keep from mouthing off:

➤ Calm yourself by taking a deep, long breath. Don't speak while you do this.

➤ Gently grit your teeth (don't hurt yourself!). This will provide you with a potent physical reminder to stay silent.

➤ If you have a drink with you, take a long, slow sip. This will physically prevent you from saying anything until you've finished.

It's Been Said
"Even the swiftest horse cannot overtake the word once spoken."
—Adage

It's Been Said
"Even a fool, when he holdeth his peace, is counted wise; and he that shutteth his lips is esteemed a man of understanding."
—Proverbs 17:28

Dealbreaker Alert
Remember to maintain good eye contact while you are deliberately remaining silent. If you look away, your opponent may think you don't really believe in what you're saying.

The Art of Extrapolation

Say you're thinking of doing some fishing but you want to be sure you'll catch more than the sun's rays. So you approach a stranger fishing off a dock and ask, "Having any luck?"

"I'm on my third carton of bait and I've been here only a half hour," the stranger replies.

So what do you think about fishing now? Just by considering the facts, you were able to draw the conclusion that the fishing is fine. That's called *extrapolation*—using facts to come to a conclusion. When you extrapolate, you discover for yourself the answer to your own questions—and so does your opponent.

Extrapolation is a powerful bargaining tool because we are always more influenced by our own conclusions than anyone else's. If you can state the facts in a way that forces your opponent to draw her own conclusion—the conclusion you want her to reach—you stand a much better chance of winning the negotiation.

Let's Talk Terms
Extrapolation is stating facts in a manner that can only lead to one inescapable conclusion.

Most of the time, when we reach a decision, we act on it. That's what happens when you permit your opponent to reach her own conclusion on what *you* want. Your opponent will quickly act on it.

Extrapolation in Action

Say you want to sell your business. You have a potential buyer who asks, "What kind of profit can this business make?"

You can offer your opinion, or the opinions of other knowledgeable people. But why not let the buyer draw her own conclusion? Why not extrapolate? Here's what you might say:

"Sales have increased an average of ten percent over the last three years, and net profits fifteen percent over that same period. The company has two new products that are hot sellers and another product in the development stage that looks very promising."

By stating facts about the business's performance, you allow the buyer to form her own conclusions about the future profit potential of your business.

A Final Word on Language

Like anything else, your command of language will only increase with practice, practice, practice. Read a wide variety of books, magazines, and newspapers so you harvest a wide vocabulary. (That way you won't be thrown when someone whispers "curable functional obsolescence" in your ear.)

Practice speaking plainly in all situations. Strive to communicate, not to impress. Learn to stay silent when you have nothing to say. You will be a more valued conversationalist—and a ferocious negotiator.

The Least You Need to Know

➤ Use simple language instead of complex terminology.

➤ If your opponent uses terms you don't understand, ask for clarification.

➤ Be as descriptive as possible. Avoid generalities.

➤ Learn to remain silent when you aren't sure what to say or when you've made a strong point.

➤ Use extrapolation to let your opponent draw her own conclusions. It is more likely to motivate your opponent than anything you say.

➤ Cultivate a wide vocabulary at every opportunity.

Chapter 6

Getting Physical: Using Body Language and Props

In This Chapter

➤ Using body language to improve your negotiation

➤ How to read your opponent's body language

➤ When and how to use props during negotiation

When James Ling decided to sell a company called Computer Technology, he expected an offer in the $60 to $65 million range. He arranged a meeting with interested buyers at Prudential Insurance. He and his associates took their seats across the bargaining table from the Prudential reps. The atmosphere was tense. Then the reps announced Prudential's opening bid: $90 million. The book *Ling*, by Stanley H. Brown (Atheneum, New York, 1972) records Ling's reaction:

"I sat there trying to organize my thoughts, because here I am with an opening bid $30 million higher than I had expected...My face was a complete mask, it showed no expression of any kind...I suggested that (my associates) and I should caucus...I did not smile as we (left the conference room)."

Let's Talk Terms
Body language is a series of purpose-ful gestures, postures, and movements that reinforce or show what you want to say.

Had Ling or any of his associates smiled, they could have completely blown the deal. A smile would have spoken as loudly as words: "Whoopee! Your offer is much higher than we expected."

Even if you're not negotiating a 90-million-dollar takeover deal, your body language is extremely important. In this chapter, you learn how to control your body language and read your opponent's body language.

Making Your Moves

The most important gesture to include in your negotiating body-language repertoire is good eye contact. No other movement conveys your honesty, sincerity, and confidence. From the minute you meet your opponent to the handshake that seals the deal, you must make and maintain eye contact. Whenever you're making a point, look directly at your opponent. If you look away, you give the impression that you don't believe in what you're saying.

Common Gestures

You can add polish to your negotiating by pairing up key phrases and ideas with a few other common—but powerful—physical gestures. Here, I've translated five phrases into their body-language equivalents. You might want to incorporate some of them into your next negotiation:

➤ "What do you think about this?" To introduce a new suggestion or appeal for help, place your hand out with the palm turned upward.

➤ "I'm passionate about this!" If you really want to convey determination to stick to a point, use a raised fist. This is a powerful gesture, so use it sparingly.

➤ "This is important." Point your index finger to call attention to an important issue.

➤ "Uh-uh." If you want to say "No way" to a suggestion or concession, make a sweeping gesture with your hand, palm facing downward.

➤ "Let's not get into this." To convey a warning or caution, place your hand straight out like a stop sign.

When it comes to your physical gestures, the most important point is to act naturally and appear relaxed. People are quick to sense artificiality and your opponent will not respond or be influenced by you if she feels she is being "put on."

Your movements, like your words, should fit the subject matter. You don't pound the desk or swing your arms when you're talking about a trivial issue. Exaggerated gestures will create an artificial impression and will also lose their impact when it comes time to use them on a larger issue.

If you're not comfortable with the technique of using your body for emphasis, you should practice before a mirror. Keep working on your moves until they look smooth, natural, and believable.

Making Your Best Poker Face

When you're negotiating, the gestures you *don't* make can be as telling as those you *do* make (remember James Ling's $30-million smile). A gasp, a flinch, or a smile can speak volumes about your position. Remember, your opponent is reading your attitude, your facial expressions, and your tone of voice—just as sharply as you are watching his.

If you find it difficult to control your facial expressions and gestures, here are a few techniques to reign yourself in:

➤ Gently grit your teeth (not too hard—it'll hurt and it'll show) to keep your face immovable.

➤ Think of something sad. This is a trick actors use when they need to shed tears during an emotional scene.

➤ Slowly take a deep breath.

➤ Make hard fists or grab the seat of your chair to tense your body and remind yourself to remain impassive. Just make sure your opponent can't see you doing this—she may misinterpret your gestures.

➤ Practice controlling your reactions in everyday life. You will find it easier to do it when you negotiate.

If harsh words are exchanged during the negotiation, don't glower for the remainder of the meeting. Express your displeasure however you have to—then move on. That's a good way to let your opponent know that you're not going to let one bad exchange stifle the entire discussion.

At the other extreme, don't go through the negotiation with a smile fixed rigidly on your face. That's unrealistic. Let your facial expressions flow naturally.

When the negotiating session is over, depart with a friendly, genuine smile and warm handshake—even if the negotiation has been tough. Don't show displeasure. A warm smile will prove your objectivity and can help smooth your way into later meetings or discussions.

What's Your Opponent's Body Language Saying?

During negotiation, it's just as important to observe what your opponent does as it is to listen to what he says. Fix your concentration on your opponent's body language—you can often pick up significant information.

So watch your opponent during discussions. Don't spend your time taking notes—only jot down the terms of agreements you've reached or information you don't want to forget. Don't look at other distractions in the office. Your opponent's facial and body expressions will be sending out all kinds of signals, and you want to be certain you're in a position to catch as many of those signals as possible and make use of them during the negotiation.

Use the following table to translate common gestures into their verbal equivalents. Just keep in mind that this is by no means infallible—like verbal language, certain gestures are used differently to mean different things by different people.

Body Language	What It Could Mean
Avoiding eye contact	Lack of confidence in bargaining position
Making excessive eye contact	Trying to bully or intimidate
Shifting eyes	Trying to deceive
Fiddling with objects, such as hair, pencils, or papers	Lack of confidence in bargaining position
Crossing and uncrossing legs	Impatient—wants to cut a deal quickly
Keeping legs or arms crossed	Not receptive to your bargaining position

Propping Yourself Up: Using Props in Negotiation

I once had a client who wanted to entice a well-known celebrity to endorse my client's business venture. I had an eye-catching mock-up of the proposed business name and logo made, which I kept under wraps during the early bargaining. Then, when my instincts told me to go for it, I unveiled the design and set it on the table for my opponent to see. Its impact was immediate. He eyed the replica closely and slowly nodded his approval. After that, we quickly reached an agreement.

In Chapter 2, I discussed the different kinds of documents that you might want to bring to the bargaining table. Any and all of the materials that you bring along with you—files, reports, pictures, diagrams, slides, artwork, videos, documents—can be used as props.

Why Use Props?

You've heard the phrase, "A picture is worth a thousand words." That's certainly true in negotiation. A single photograph or document can make or break your case more effectively than anything you could possibly say. There are many benefits to using props:

Let's Talk Terms
Props are any materials, documents, charts, or accessories that help you demonstrate and strengthen your bargaining position.

➤ *Props legitimize and document your position.* If you're asking for a raise, for example, and one of your key arguments is the phenomenal sales you're responsible for, bring in a sales report and go over it with your boss. Then leave the report with the soaring company profit figures in plain view while you negotiate. Throughout your negotiation, it will serve as a constant, silent testament to your contributions to the company.

➤ *Props dramatize your bargaining position.* That's why lawyers who prosecute murder trials always try to get graphic photographs of the victims and crime scene admitted into evidence. Those pictures convey the viciousness of the crime to the jury more effectively than anything anyone can say. You can get the same result when you use props when you negotiate.

➤ *Props allow you to concentrate on something else.* In the heat of negotiation, you can't keep track of myriad financial figures or complex legalese. Props can communicate and exhibit that information for you. They free you to focus on other aspects of the bargaining.

➤ *Props break your opponent's negotiating momentum.* When you display a prop, your opponent will react immediately. She'll focus on it and lose concentration on her own position.

When and How to Use Props

Because they wield so much power, props must be used carefully and delicately. Here are a few pointers:

➤ Be intimately familiar with any props you bring. You don't want a prop to backfire. For example, if you're bringing a contract or warranty, read the entire document thoroughly—not just the sections that bolster your side. A skillful opponent might discover a clause or condition lurking in the small print that works against you. Similarly, check all video and audio tapes, brochures, and so on before displaying them at the bargaining table.

➤ If you're unsure about using a prop, put yourself in your opponent's shoes and ask yourself whether the exhibit would have a dramatic, favorable influence on you. If the answer is "Yes," then use it.

➤ Similarly, always have a definite objective when you use props. Be sure your props will boost your bargaining position. If you're not sure, don't use them because their impact on your opponent can be strong.

➤ If you use props, make sure they are top quality. Your opponent won't take you seriously if your case relies on miscollated copies or a fuzzy videotape.

When Should You Haul Out Your Props?

You want to produce your props at that point in the bargaining when you feel they will have the greatest impact and influence on your opponent. The more bargaining experience you gain, the easier it'll be for you to decide the best time to use your exhibits.

When your prop is a key part of your bargaining position—like those impressive sales figures—display it throughout the entire negotiation. Refer to it frequently. The prop's presence will reinforce your position, and the longer your opponent looks at it, the more convincing and formidable it becomes.

If your prop is only a small part of your bargaining position, display it for only that part. Then tuck it away out of your opponent's view. You don't want your opponent distracted by your prop once it's served its purpose.

When You Negotiate Over a Prop

When you are negotiating to buy or sell something—property, a house, or a car, for example—the object itself can serve as a prop. I once negotiated the price of a piece of land and had a written appraisal—my first prop—which my opponent came to my office to discuss. At our meeting, I gave my opponent a copy of the document and explained it in detail, page by page.

We then left the office and visited the property, where I once again listed the highlights of the appraisal as we both looked at the land—my second prop. I was able to drive my point home through three separate channels: my words, the appraisal, and the view of the property itself. By using props so powerfully, I convinced my opponent to accept my value of the property.

In some cases, props are the only way to win your case. I once negotiated a controversy over the quality of food that was being created for a proposed large restaurant chain. One side claimed the food was fine—the other side said it simply wasn't good enough. A food expert, who was called in to make taste samplings, concluded that the food was indeed okay. In this case, a single taste was worth a thousand words.

The Least You Need to Know

➤ Use body language to underline your arguments when you negotiate.

➤ Your body language should be relaxed and appropriate.

➤ Control your facial expressions so you don't give any extra information to your opponent.

➤ Watch your opponent for telltale gestures and expressions that may reveal his position.

➤ Use props such as documents or videos to legitimize, dramatize, and emphasize your bargaining position.

➤ Only use props that are professional looking and that you are entirely familiar with.

➤ If your prop is an important part of your bargaining position, display it throughout the entire negotiation. If not, put it away once you've used it to make your point.

Chapter 7

It's All in the Timing: Pacing and Deadlines

In This Chapter

➤ Why good timing is important

➤ Why good timing is especially critical when you make an offer or counteroffer

➤ How you can regain your timing if you've lost it

➤ How deadlines increase your negotiating power

➤ Setting, extending, and avoiding deadlines

I once spent several heated sessions negotiating with a business colleague. After our third meeting, he promised to call within the week to set up yet another conference. I didn't hear from him for three weeks. When he finally did call, he said he wanted to meet that very day.

In my experience, people who are anxious to meet right away are usually prepared to the hilt and raring to negotiate. All my instincts said, "Stall him!" So I did. I begged off and suggested that we meet the following week. This took the edge off my opponent, bought me a little time to prepare, and put the negotiation back in balance.

Timing has a crucial impact on your negotiating position. Appear too eager and you may get taken for a ride. Let a negotiation slide and your opponent may find a better deal elsewhere. While it's impossible to teach a good sense of timing, it does gets better with experience. In this chapter, I show you how to get time on your side when you negotiate.

The Importance of Good Timing

The first question of timing is raised when you decide when to meet. I've discussed this a bit in Chapter 4. If your opponent is anxious to negotiate, you can assume she is very confident of her ability to win. If that's the case, delay the bargaining, because the timing is not favorable for you. Give your opponent a plausible reason for postponing—such as saying you need more time to prepare, or that you have another meeting. That throws off her timing and increases your bargaining power.

If your opponent sounds reluctant to meet, press as hard as you can (without getting offensive) to meet sooner rather than later. You want to use your opponent's unpreparedness to your advantage.

It's Been Said
"Every successful person I have ever known has had it… it is that instinct or ability to sense and seize the right moment without wavering or playing it safe…" —Moss Hart

Once you are at the bargaining table, you'll have to ask yourself, "Is this the best time to say or do what I want to?" If your instincts are saying, "Yes," then go for it. In most cases, your timing will be right.

One of the best ways you can sharpen your sense of timing is to think over every one of your negotiations. Ask yourself if what you said and did had the maximum impact and influence on your opponent. If you're candid with yourself, this analysis process will help you hone your sense of timing.

Good Timing for Offers or Counteroffers

An *offer* is the first proposal made, either by you to your opponent or from your opponent to you. A *counteroffer* is a reply to the initial offer or to another counteroffer.

I'll get into offers and counteroffers in more detail in Chapter 21. For now, you should know that *when* you make an offer or counteroffer will affect how your opponent receives it. If you make an offer prematurely, you'll get a rejection even if your proposal is reasonable because your opponent won't be mentally ready to accept it.

There's no set formula you can use to determine the best time to make an offer or counteroffer. You've just got to trust your instincts. If you get that gut feeling that the time is right, go for it. Make an offer your opponent can't refuse.

You'll immediately know from your opponent's reaction if your timing was right. If your opponent is receptive—great! Press on with the bargaining. If you get a negative reaction, back off and continue. You may have to throw in some concessions or scale back your expectations—that's okay. Don't quit, be patient, and don't get rattled. As long as you're still bargaining, you have a chance to win.

It's Been Said
"Experience is not what happens to a man. It is what man does with what happens to him."
—Aldous Huxley

Experience, again, is your best teacher. The more you negotiate and review your negotiating experiences, the better your timing will become.

Help! I've Lost My Timing!

When you lose your timing you'll know it. Nothing you say is well received and nothing you suggest is accepted. You're on the defensive. A little voice in your mind asks, "How did I get into this and how can I get out?"

The best way is to stop negotiating. Ask for a break: a short one if you can pull yourself together quickly, a long one if you feel you need more time. Use the break time to think about what you said and did and why it's not working. Prepare some new suggestions that may get the negotiating ball rolling again. In most cases, you'll be able to figure out your mistakes and how to correct them.

Negotiating on a Deadline

Nobody likes deadlines. In negotiation, setting a deadline is like sticking a ticking time bomb under your opponent. Deadlines are powerful motivators, and, if you've been a sharp negotiator, your opponent will be motivated to act in your favor.

Use deadlines liberally when you negotiate—but only if you're prepared to live with the consequences should you receive no response by the deadline. If you're not, don't set a deadline until you're confident you can live without the deal.

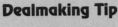

Dealmaking Tip

Real estate negotiation is a fertile area in which deadlines play an important role. When negotiating real estate deals, I rarely give my opponents more than three to five days to accept an offer or counteroffer. That makes my opponent come to a decision quickly, and limits the amount of time she has to shop around for a better deal.

Putting Your Opponent on a Deadline

When you set deadlines, fear becomes your bargaining ally. Your opponent is afraid of losing the deal, losing the money, losing your business. Deadlines play on that fear in two ways:

➤ *Deadlines reduce your opponent's options.* If you don't set a deadline, you're giving your opponent an opportunity to shop around for a better deal. If he finds one, you're out. That puts you in a defensive bargaining position.

Dealmaking Tip
When you bargain with an opponent who doesn't set deadlines when you feel he should, you'll immediately know your opponent is not experienced in the art of negotiation.

➤ *Deadlines give you greater bargaining flexibility.* Say a number of buyers are interested in buying your home. You receive a firm offer from one buyer, but you want to hear some other offers before you seal a deal. So you make a counteroffer with a five-day deadline. Your deadline allows you to plan a definite course of action if the five-day period expires with no acceptance. You can immediately look for other buyers. Or you can accept offers from other buyers you're already dealing with. You then wait for the five-day period to expire before you act on any other offers.

Dealbreaker Alert

The laws in most states say that an offer or counteroffer is open for a reasonable time if no deadline is set at the time the offer is made. What "a reasonable time" is depends on the facts and circumstances of the particular case. Making offers or counteroffers without fixing a definite deadline for acceptance, then, is a risky business.

How to Determine the Deadline Period

Set the shortest deadline you can reasonably justify. No one likes tight deadlines—if your deadline is too short you can make your opponent angry. But a deadline that seems too remote won't motivate your opponent to act quickly.

You may have to adjust the length of your deadline in light of the particular circumstances of your negotiation. Factor in the personality, experience, and competence of your opponent. Usually, the more experienced and competent he is, the shorter your deadline can be. Your opponent may protest, but he will expect a short deadline.

Always be prepared to offer a legitimate reason why you set your deadline. You can say you need time to deal with other interested parties (that's a good approach because it creates fear of loss in your opponent), or you have other business to handle and want to settle the issue as soon as possible.

Dealmaking Tip
If your opponent says your deadline is too short, ask him to explain why. If the explanation is reasonable (he will be traveling, has a family emergency, or must consult with others), then extend your deadline.

Dealmaking Tip

When you explain the reason for your tight deadline, you diminish the risk that your opponent will be irritated by it.

Should You Grant an Extension?

There are two very important rules you should follow when it comes to extending deadlines:

➤ When you set a deadline, be absolutely certain that you can live with it.

➤ Do not extend your deadline unless there is a legitimate reason to do so.

The two rules work together. If you set a deadline you can't live with, you'll have to extend it for no good reason. If you do that, your opponent won't take any of your deadlines seriously, which means you'll lose substantial bargaining power.

If you've set a reasonable deadline and it expires, you must be fully prepared to walk away from the negotiation. If your opponent gives you a legitimate reason for needing an extension (such as personal issues, the need for more information, or the need to firm up financing), you're safe to extend your deadline. In that case, your new deadline will still be taken seriously.

Dealing With Deadlines Placed on You

If your opponent sets a deadline and you can meet it, meet it. If you can't, ask for an extension well in advance of the deadline. If you wait until the last minute, you'll have a lot of anxiety wondering if you are going to get the extra time you need.

Dealmaking Tip
Always explain to your opponent why you need more time. The more you can justify an extension, the more likely it is you'll get one.

If your opponent does agree to give you more time, ask for more time than you need. That way, if your opponent gives you less time than you've asked for, you're still ahead of the game.

If your opponent flatly refuses to give you more time and you can't make a decision without it, *insist* that you need an extension. Make it clear that the deal can't be settled unless you have more time. In most cases, you'll get what you're asking for.

Dealmaking Tip

It's human nature to prefer to procrastinate—to put off doing something until we absolutely must. That's why negotiating deadlines are so useful—they force both you and your opponent to make a decision and take action by a specified time.

Avoid Imposing Deadlines on Yourself

Be very careful not to hurt your bargaining position by setting deadlines on yourself. Even a casual, innocent remark about your future plans may bind you into a deadline.

For example, if you tip off your opponent that you have another appointment or that you must catch a flight, you're setting a deadline on yourself. A skillful opponent will use anything that puts a time constraint on you. I have often dragged out a meeting until my opponent's self-imposed deadline approached—knowing that time would motivate my opponent to cave in and give me what I wanted.

Dealbreaker Alert
Self-imposed deadlines have the same impact on you that your deadlines have on your opponent.

Dealbreaker Alert

Home sales are a fertile area for self-imposed deadlines. Many times, the homeowners will reveal that they need to move right away, either because their new home is finished or they have to relocate for their jobs. If you're the buyer in that situation, time is on your side. If you're the seller, don't admit to the buyers or to your agent that you have pressing deadlines. It will make you vulnerable to a less-than-ideal deal.

If your opponent is a skilled negotiator, he will probe to see if you have any self-imposed deadlines. He'll usually ask questions like, "How's business?" or "Are you making any money?" They may seem like innocent questions, but don't be caught off-guard.

He may be fishing to see if you have any travel, personal, or business commitments that impose a deadline on you. When you answer those questions, be brief. Short responses don't disclose any of your plans or commitments and thus don't reveal any deadlines that you have to meet.

I probe for self-imposed deadlines every time I negotiate. Sometimes I come up empty-handed. But many times I hit the jackpot and use my opponent's self-imposed deadline to my advantage.

The Least You Need to Know

➤ Always think about *when* you should say and do what you intend to say and do when you're bargaining. If you time it right, your odds of succeeding will be substantially increased.

➤ The more bargaining experience you gain, the more you'll develop good timing.

➤ If you feel you've lost your timing, ask for an immediate recess. Pull yourself together, think about what happened and why, and in most cases you'll figure out what went wrong and how you can correct it.

➤ Deadlines increase your negotiating power because they reduce your opponent's options and increase your options. Set the shortest deadlines you can reasonably justify.

➤ Be sure you can live with any deadlines you impose. Don't extend your deadlines unless there's a legitimate reason to do so.

➤ If you can meet deadlines imposed on you by your opponent—do it. If not, ask for an extension as soon as possible and always ask for more time than you need.

➤ Be careful not to impose deadlines on yourself, and don't admit to any self-imposed deadlines.

Chapter 8

Questions, Questions, and More Questions

In This Chapter

➤ Why questions are an important part of the bargaining process

➤ How to use questions when you negotiate

➤ The different types of questions

➤ How each type of question works in negotiation

How do major political or social personalities fend off the media during a scandal? Usually, with two simple yet suggestive words: "No comment."

Unless you're used to getting hounded by reporters, I'll bet you do the opposite. You probably answer questions even when you shouldn't, or don't want to. Most people do. (How many times have you wanted to tell a nagging relative or nosy neighbor to butt out of your business, but just didn't know how?)

The same thing happens when you negotiate. Most inexperienced negotiators will answer questions even when they shouldn't. By asking questions liberally, you can boost your negotiating position. In this chapter, I show you how to ask all the right questions when you negotiate.

Why Ask Why? The Benefits of Using Questions

Questions are excellent probing tools for two reasons:

Dealmaking Tip
A timely question can cast doubt on your opponent's bargaining position because it implies that you're not convinced it's a valid position.

➤ They help you discover information that only your opponent knows, or that is otherwise very difficult for you to get.

➤ They give you more control over the tone and flow of the negotiation.

There are several kinds of questions, and each has a different purpose and place in negotiation. Over the following pages I'll describe each one. Before we begin: Any questions?

Sizing Up the Situation: General Questions

Dealmaking Tip
Ask questions frequently when you negotiate. If your questions are important, write them out beforehand to help you phrase them so they have the greatest impact and get the best results.

General questions are useful for probing for new facts and information. The best time to use them is during the early stages of the bargaining, while you and your opponent are still getting to know each other, before the terms have been laid out on the bargaining table. Your opponent will answer most, if not all, of your general questions with no suspicions at this point. So ask general questions freely.

If you reread Chapters 2 and 3 on researching before you negotiate, you may be so well prepared for the negotiation that you don't have any general questions to ask. But ask anyway! The way your opponent answers may give you new insights into her personality.

Examples of General Questions

The possibilities of general questions are endless. But here are some examples of questions you might want to ask.

During a business negotiation:

➤ "So, Company Z used to handle this account for you. What did you think of them?"

➤ "How long have you been in this business? With this company?"

When buying a home:

➤ "What's the neighborhood like? How are the schools? The recreation?"

➤ "What kind of condition is the house in?"

➤ "Why are the owners selling?"

When selling a home:

➤ "What are you looking for in a home?"

➤ "Are you interested in this neighborhood because it's near such good schools?"

The Risk of Asking General Questions

You should abandon general questions as the bargaining unfolds. For one thing, by asking more general questions you run the risk of reopening issues that were already agreed upon.

More importantly, if you keep asking general questions as the negotiation gets specific, your opponent will wonder how prepared you are—and whether you know anything about the subject at hand. She won't go along with you on anything if she feels you don't know what you're talking about.

Or she might see a more sinister motive in your general questions. She may conclude that your bargaining position is weak and that you're trying to strengthen it by pumping her for more information.

Dealbreaker Alert
All of your questions should have an objective. If you ask a pointless question, your opponent may give an answer that bolsters his bargaining position. This can put you on the defensive and force you to lose control of the negotiation.

Getting into Specifics: Specific Questions

Unlike general questions, *specific questions* call for fairly confined answers. You can use specific questions at any point during a negotiation, but they're best asked in the later stages, when you're more apt to know exactly what you're after when asking.

Watch how you phrase your specific questions. The more precise your question, the better the chance you'll get a precise answer—without exposing your bargaining strategy or opening yourself up to other questions.

Say you're in the market to buy property and build a restaurant. If you're concerned about zoning, you should ask, "Is the property fully zoned for use as a restaurant?" Not, "What's the property's zoning?" The first question is more likely to get you the information you want.

Getting Instant Results: Leading Questions

Leading questions are simply statements turned into questions. Leading questions always call for "yes" answers. When you ask a leading question, you already know what response you expect to get from your opponent. Leading questions help you maintain control of the bargaining, and may push your negotiating momentum further along.

Examples of Leading Questions

You form leading questions by twisting around your sentence. Take a look at the following examples:

Leading question: "It's a very profitable company, isn't it?"

What you want your opponent to admit: "It's a very profitable company."

Leading question: "He was driving very fast, wasn't he?"

What you want your opponent to admit: "He was driving very fast."

Leading question: "I've done an excellent job and really earned a raise, haven't I?"

What you want your opponent to admit: "You've earned a raise."

Leading questions that call for a "yes" response from your opponent are powerful not only because they call forth the answer you want to hear, but also because they put your opponent in a "yes" mood—exactly the mood you want your opponent to be in.

Take the question, "I've earned a raise, haven't I?" If your boss says "Yes," it's going to be more difficult for her to weasel her way out of giving you a raise, unless there are major company problems that prevent *anyone* from getting a raise.

The Risk of Asking Leading Questions

You've probably seen more than one courtroom drama where the star witness shocks the court with a surprise confession that no one—not even the lawyers—saw coming. That's the risk of asking a leading question: you'll bomb big-time if you're not sure what the answer will be. You'll automatically go on the defensive, scrambling to regain some control, and you'll lower your chances of winning the negotiation.

Just picture how quickly your campaign for a raise will come crashing down if you say, "I've earned a raise, haven't I?" and your boss says, "Frankly, Snively, you haven't," and then launches into a list of reasons why. Even a master negotiator would be hard-pressed to recover from a blow like that.

It's Been Said
"The man who is afraid of asking is ashamed of learning."
—Danish proverb

Getting Suggestive: Suggestive Questions

As the name implies, embedded in *suggestive questions* is a specific course of action or a suggestion. For example, "Don't you think it's better to sign the contract now?" or "Wouldn't it be best to give me my money back now?" or "Isn't it a good time to give me a raise?" are suggestive questions.

In all of these suggestive questions, your opponent must either commit himself to the course of action suggested in your question or explain why not. If he agrees with your suggestion, congratulations—you've won. If he tries to explain away your suggestion, he has to go on the defensive. So any way you cut it, suggestive questions are excellent bargaining tools. Use them often.

Retail stores are hotbeds of suggestive questions. Just think of all the times you've shopped for a suit or dress, only to have the salesperson say, "How about this shirt to go with it?"

Dealmaking Tip
Use suggestive questions when you're asking your opponent something delicate and don't want to alienate or anger him.

If the salesperson asked a leading question, he could say, "You can use this new shirt to go with it, can't you?" But more than likely, that approach wouldn't work. A leading question feels more aggressive and bullying than a suggestive question.

Getting a Favorable Response: Obvious Questions

They appear similar to leading questions, but *obvious questions* are designed to get a favorable response because your opponent doesn't want to look stupid even though he may not know the correct answer.

By definition, questions that call for obvious answers have to relate to matters of common knowledge. If you're negotiating a raise, you might cry, "Doesn't everyone know that the cost of living has gone up?" If you're trying to buy a home, you might say, "Don't we all know it's a buyer's market?" Even if your opponent doesn't know a buyer's market from a supermarket, he will still answer—just so he doesn't look stupid.

Dealmaking Tip

Use questions that call for obvious answers liberally when you bargain. Not only do they put your opponent in an agreeable mood, but they also provide you with good negotiating momentum.

Coffee, Tea, or Me: Questions That Require a Choice

The alternatives you present when asking these *choice questions* should all be favorable to you. "Would you give me that sofa and chair combination for seven hundred dollars, or the other living room set for six hundred?" "Would you rather give me my bonus in one lump sum at the end of the year or in quarterly payments?" "Would you prefer to do your homework before dinner or after?"

Dealmaking Tip Using choice questions is a very good tactic when your opponent is evasive and you want to pin him down.

Notice how the choices in all the three questions are favorable to you. You'll take either living room set, as long as your price is met. You're after a bonus and you don't care whether it's paid annually or quarterly. You don't care when your child does her homework—as long as it gets done.

If the salesperson tries to sell you the imitation-leather sofa, or your boss attempts to switch the subject back to the Smithers account, or your child still evades the homework subject, your choice questions will pin them down.

Maintaining Control: Successive Questions

Successive questions are excellent for maintaining control and developing positive bargaining momentum.

Say the lease on your apartment is about to run out. You want to renew, but at a lower rent. Here's how you use successive questions to help get what you want:

"Why shouldn't I get a rent reduction? Haven't I been a good tenant? Haven't I kept the place in perfect shape? Haven't I cooperated with you every time you needed to get into the apartment? Shouldn't all of that be worth something? Don't you think it's fair and reasonable to give me a ten-percent rent reduction?"

Notice how your questions build up to your final question, the grand finale, the pièce de résistance—your ultimate objective, which is a lower rent. You can add as many questions as you like—building successive questions is like piling layers on lasagna. (Just make sure you don't run out of breath before you get through your questions.)

Your purpose when using successive questions is not to bully, annoy, or intimidate. It's to make your case without being interrupted so the total sum of your questions has a much greater impact.

Dealmaking Tip
Successive questions are excellent tools to keep the bargaining momentum flowing in your favor. By the time you get to your final question, it will be very difficult for your opponent to resist.

No Comment—How to Avoid Answering Questions

If your opponent asks you a question you feel is appropriate, don't hesitate to answer. If you refuse, your opponent may become suspicious of your motives. She may also begin to resent you for appearing uncooperative.

But you'll sometimes encounter questions that you shouldn't answer. Here are some tactful approaches you can use to dodge a question without turning off your opponent:

➤ *Plead irrelevance.* Say something like, "I'm not sure how that question fits in here," or "I don't see where you're coming from." Your response is mild and won't turn your opponent off—but it may get your opponent to drop the question.

➤ *Plead ignorance.* Simply say that you don't know the answer. Realize, though, that with this approach you risk looking uninformed or unprepared.

➤ *Take the fifth.* Tactfully suggest that the question calls for information you'd rather not disclose—at least not at this point in the bargaining process.

➤ *Answer that it's too personal.* If the question calls for personal information you'd rather not disclose, say so. Your opponent should respect your right to privacy.

➤ *Answer with your own question.* Answering your opponent's question with a question of your own is an excellent way to avoid the question and regain control of the bargaining momentum.

The Least You Need to Know

➤ Questions are excellent probing tools that help you to get information you might not otherwise have access to.

➤ Always have an objective when you ask questions.

➤ General questions are best at the beginning of the bargaining. Specific questions call for more confined answers and are useful at any stage of the bargaining.

➤ Leading questions seek a "yes" answer and put your opponent in a "yes" mood. Never ask them unless you are certain your opponent's answer will be "yes."

➤ Use suggestive questions and questions that require a choice to get a commitment from your opponent.

➤ Questions that call for obvious answers put your opponent in an agreeable mood and give you good bargaining momentum. Use them liberally.

➤ Successive questions help you to control the bargaining. Ask them without pausing because you don't want your opponent to reply until you finish.

Chapter 9

Using Correspondence Effectively When You Negotiate

A client of mine once negotiated a large and intricate deal with a group of business people anxious to seal an agreement. At the eleventh hour, however, he reviewed the terms and decided that he just couldn't go through with the arrangement. He asked me if I could help untangle the situation.

As I reviewed his case, I realized that if my client didn't make his wishes clear, he could easily get slapped with a number of lawsuits.

I drafted a letter on his behalf and spent literally three days pruning and fine-tuning it. I tried to imagine how my opponents would feel, and what they would likely do when they received it.

When I was finally convinced that I had the letter right, I sent it out. Then I waited—and waited—and waited some more. Finally, I received a response: They were not going to pursue the deal, or prosecute my client.

Correspondence can play a powerful role in the bargaining process. In this chapter, I show you how to prepare and present professional-looking correspondence.

The Uses of Correspondence

Correspondence and paperwork serve many purposes throughout the negotiation process, from the opening bargaining through the offer and counteroffer stages and on to closing.

Opening the Negotiation

Many negotiations, particularly business negotiations, begin with a written offer or other bargaining "position paper." This document sets forth the issues you want to negotiate, and your hopes for the negotiation process.

If you have to prepare a position paper, craft it carefully, because it will set the tone and direction for the upcoming negotiation. Also, if any expectations or promises are set forth in the opening paper (for example, stipulations as to fees or legal rights), you'll be held to them, and it will be very difficult to back out once you've committed yourself in writing.

Here are some pointers on how to prepare effective written offers or other opening position papers:

➤ Keep them brief. The less you write, the less you are committed to.

➤ Be concise.

➤ If you're in doubt about a particular term or proposal, leave it out! You can always raise the issue later.

➤ Arrange your ideas and positions so that each point flows logically from the previous one. This avoids confusion about what you've written.

➤ Put yourself in your opponent's shoes and read your letter. How does it sound? Does it make sense? This will help clarify your writing.

Clearing the Air

I'm sure you've heard the saying, "Don't make a mountain out of a molehill." That often happens when you're bargaining. Simple issues snowball into complicated ones.

Correspondence can be the perfect vehicle to get back to basics. By outlining and organizing the issue on paper, you can separate the crucial issues from the negligible ones.

For example, I once had a client who wanted to rezone his property. What began as a simple request turned into a bureaucratic nightmare as numerous government agencies, planning commissions, and local community boards all got involved, expressing competing viewpoints, interests, and requirements. I had to craft a simple letter that stated the current status of the request to bring everyone involved in the negotiation back on track.

Plus, by reporting on the issues that are important to you first, you can control the direction of the negotiation. You can de-emphasize issues that are not important to you by placing them in parentheses or mentioning them in a brief postscript.

You can also de-emphasize any matters you feel are unimportant by using language such as "I place little emphasis on…" or "I see little merit in…," going on to explain why you feel that way.

Getting It in Writing

The printed or written word lends credibility. People are much more likely to believe what they see and read than what they hear.

Following up your discussions with a letter detailing the issues resolved is an excellent way to avoid misunderstanding. This approach is especially useful when the negotiation is complicated or drawn out over more than one bargaining session. Details can be interpreted differently, or perhaps even forgotten. Your understanding of the agreements reached can be different than your opponent's understanding. Restating your interpretation can head off serious problems down the road when you're anxious to close the negotiation.

Blazing a Paper Trail

Not only do follow-up letters clarify issues, they also serve as official proof of promises made, terms agreed on, and actions taken. Sign and date all your correspondence, and keep a file of every letter you send out and receive. You never know when you'll need it.

Regular mail, Federal Express, UPS, faxes, and electronic mail (e-mail) are fine for sending standard documents and letters. If you are sending particularly sensitive or crucial documents, the U.S. Postal Service offers several options that guarantee your letters will get where they are going:

➤ *Certified mail* provides you with a mailing receipt, and a record of delivery is kept at the recipient's post office.

➤ *Registered mail* is regarded by the Postal Service as its most secure mailing option.

➤ *Restricted delivery* means that delivery is made only to the addressee or to someone who has written authorization to receive mail for the addressee.

Looking Good on Paper: The Qualities of Effective Correspondence

How you present yourself in writing is as important as how you present yourself in person. I'm amazed at how many people still submit handwritten letters or badly smudged Xeroxed copies. If you want to be taken seriously on paper, you should follow a few basic rules:

➤ *Be accurate.* Proofread everything you send to your opponent—twice. In negotiation, even one little word can make a substantial difference. If you want to inform your opponent that her offer is not acceptable, but leave out the word *not*, you've got a lot of explaining to do.

➤ *Be neat.* Type your letter to your opponent. If you want to add a personal touch, write a handwritten note on the page (be sure your handwriting is clear).

➤ *Use a conservative design, with a classic typeface and generous margins.* This isn't the time to display your hip sensibilities or funky design style.

➤ *Use highlighting elements like bold, underline, or exclamation points sparingly.* If you emphasize too many points in your letter, you will appear obnoxious, strident, or too opinionated.

➤ *Avoid jokes, sarcasm, or irony in your letter—unless you're certain the recipient will understand and appreciate your humor.* Your letter won't be able to communicate the subtle voice intonations and gestures that signify you're just kidding.

➤ *Be prompt.* By delaying correspondence, you will appear unprofessional, disorganized, or not confident in your negotiating position.

Using Forms

A number of matters you negotiate will involve printed or standard documents such as apartment leases, car leases, service contracts, repair contracts, or employment contracts. The use of forms in particular negotiations is covered in more detail in Part 7, "Everyday

Negotiating Situations." For now, there are some general rules you should follow when you are confronted with a printed or standard document:

➤ Never sign a document on the spot. Get a copy early on in the bargaining if you can so you (or someone you trust) can review the document in detail. (Be sure to read the fine print.) If you are apartment hunting, for example, you might want to pick up a standard lease in a stationery store. Then, when you are presented with a lease to sign, you will have a rough idea what will be in it.

➤ As you negotiate, make notes on the document so you have a quick and accurate reference to work from. If you aren't comfortable marking up the original, take a copy and use that.

➤ Printed documents are often worded in dense legalese. Don't let that intimidate you! Seek an explanation of any language you're unsure about.

➤ Pay attention to any preexisting conditions that may affect the terms of the document. For example, if an apartment lease states that you are financially responsible for any damages you cause, you should check the apartment before you move in and document any damages (holes, stains, faulty heating or plumbing, and so on) that are already there. Otherwise, under the terms of the lease, you could be held responsible for damages you didn't even cause.

➤ Realize that no document is official until all concerned parties have signed it. And oftentimes, any changes, additions, or deletions marked on a document also have to be initialed by all parties before they are official. Everyone involved in the negotiation should have an identical copy of the form.

➤ All parties should keep a signed copy of the document for their records.

Who Should Receive Your Correspondence?

If you bargain with more than one opponent, send the original to the "yes" person and copies to everyone else involved in the negotiation.

If you are not bargaining directly with the "yes" person, send the original to the person you are bargaining with and a copy to the "yes" person.

If your negotiation is controversial and you're not sure how it will turn out, your written correspondence should contain a reference that you have sent a copy to your lawyer (if you are using one). This lets your opponent know that you're serious and that the negotiation is being monitored by a professional.

The Least You Need to Know

➤ Correspondence helps you control the bargaining process.

➤ Use correspondence to clarify your position and create a paper trail of promises and accountability.

➤ Your correspondence should be neat, error-free, and timely.

➤ Send the original correspondence to the person you are bargaining with directly. Send copies to anyone else involved in the negotiation.

➤ Send a copy of your correspondence to your lawyer when you feel you need additional bargaining leverage.

Chapter 10

Tricks of the Trade: My Top Negotiating Techniques

In previous chapters I've shown you how to use the powers of communication (both verbal and non-verbal), questions, correspondence, and timing to boost your negotiating prowess. Now I'd like to tip you off to some of my favorite negotiating techniques and how each one works.

When you prepare to bargain, decide which of these techniques will work the best to persuade your opponent. Use as many and as often as you feel is necessary—and at every window of opportunity, no matter how small.

Dealmaking Tip
Act naturally when you use negotiating techniques. That gives them greater impact. If you're nervous and uptight, your opponent will become suspicious and won't respond the way you expect. That can hurt your bargaining position and your confidence.

The "Building Block" Technique

This technique is designed to impress your opponent with your preparation and knowledge of the negotiating situation. With the "Building Block" technique, you build your case with facts and figures, thus bolstering your position (and your image) in your opponent's eyes.

Dealbreaker Alert

The "Building Block" technique requires patience. Don't be too anxious to reveal your supporting facts too quickly. Dribble them out like drops from a leaky faucet.

If the bargaining lasts for only one meeting (as many will), your goal is to parcel out your facts throughout the entire meeting rather than all at once. That makes it appear as if you have much more supportive information than is actually the case.

For longer negotiations, parcel out your facts over several bargaining sessions. The cumulative effect leaves your opponent with the impression that your bargaining position is stronger than it really is.

Whether you're parceling out your facts over one bargaining session or several sessions, always start with your strongest facts, but keep some in reserve. Then go with your weaker facts and finish with your remaining stronger facts. The effect is like a roller coaster ride. This approach leaves a strong impact because we tend to retain the first and last pieces of information the longest. Everything in between is largely forgotten.

The "Vinegar and Honey" Technique

"Vinegar and honey" situations occur every day. Recently, I was on a flight that was about to land when the pilot announced that there would be an hour's delay because of heavy traffic at the airport. All of the passengers grumbled and settled in for a long, boring wait.

A few minutes later, the pilot announced the delay had been cut to a half hour. Five minutes later, the pilot gave us the good news that we'd been cleared for immediate landing. We were thrilled with the news—even though we were already late.

By discouraging your opponent with bad news (the vinegar) you then make the good news (the honey) seem even sweeter—even if the good news isn't as good as your opponent expected.

A Taste of Vinegar and Honey

Say you're a boss and a valued employee asks for a ten-percent raise. While ten percent is too high, you're secretly willing and able to give him five percent because you want to keep him on your team. So you don't reject the ten percent outright. You say, "Oh, I really don't know… There's a wage freeze on the entire company, and as much as I'd like to give you a raise, I just don't know what I'll be able to do. But let me see what I can do."

Your employee is obviously going to be disappointed because you haven't agreed to the raise on the spot. But you haven't closed the door entirely. You reschedule a later meeting.

At the next meeting, you begin with the bad news. You say, "Well, I really tried, but I just couldn't get that ten-percent raise for you. There was just no way." At this point, your employee may be worried that absolutely *no* raise is forthcoming. Then comes the honey: "But I did manage to get five percent for you." Your employee will be elated, even though he didn't get the entire raise he was asking for.

If you're the one asking for the raise, you reverse the process. If your goal is a ten-percent raise, you ask for twenty and then, when your boss gives you a sob story about why twenty percent is too high, you gradually scale back until you're at your final ten-percent target.

> **Dealmaking Tip**
> Act very naturally when you're using the "Vinegar and Honey" technique. You don't want to reveal that your secret objective is any different than the one you verbally propose.

Avoid Large Concessions

The "Vinegar and Honey" technique works best when you make concessions in small increments. If you make a large concession all at once ("What's that, Mr. Smith? No twenty-percent raise? Well, in that case, one percent is fine!") you can devastate your entire case (more on this in Chapter 21). Smaller concessions are more convincing and leave you more room to negotiate.

The "Exhausting" Technique

I once handled a negotiation in which my opponent was after more than $13 million. I knew I faced a difficult battle—it usually is, when there's that much money involved. I decided to use the "Exhausting" technique.

> **Dealmaking Tip**
> Be patient when using the "Exhausting" technique. If your confidence or concentration wavers, take a break. Use recesses as part of your bargaining strategy.

I arranged to conduct the bargaining over a number of smaller sessions rather than one or two drawn-out meetings. My game plan was to get one small concession at every meeting. We had six meetings, and I did get a small concession at each one. Finally, the $13 million was reduced to less than $1 million.

When you use the "Exhausting" technique, there's always the risk that your opponent will threaten to break off the bargaining out of sheer frustration. For that reason, this technique works best when you're bargaining about something that your opponent can't afford to walk away from, such as selling a home or settling a customer dispute.

The "Gear-Shifting" Technique

Gear shifting means changing from one issue to another the way a truck driver shifts gears when driving up a steep hill. When you use this technique, your opponent never knows when you are about to shift to other issues. This keeps your opponent off-balance and swings the advantage to you.

Let's say you're negotiating to buy widgets for your company. The representative from Wonder Widgets promises you a discount if you buy a 1,000-lot case, which is more widgets than you could ever possibly need. He can also guarantee delivery by October 1, but you want your widgets at least a month sooner. Finally, he wants the bill settled with 15-day net terms. Your company's accounting department doesn't usually operate that way.

You have three items on your negotiating agenda. This is a classic case where you can successfully use the "Gear-Shifting" technique to your advantage. Here's how you would use it in this situation.

Start with the amount of widgets you need, but don't agree to a final amount. Then shift to the delivery-date issue. You consult your calendar and start tossing out possible dates by which you need the widgets. Leaving that issue unresolved, you finally turn to the payment terms and again, confuse the issue without settling anything.

Soon, your opponent will be disoriented and receptive to any reasonable offer. You then tailor your proposals on each issue to what you want.

The "Conduit" Technique

In Chapter 3, I told you how to prepare for a negotiation in which you would be facing several opponents, including the "yes" person. In this situation, you might want to pull out the "Conduit" technique from your negotiating arsenal.

A conduit is a channel for conveying something. When you can't persuade the "yes" person, you focus your efforts on persuading his colleagues and using them to help you persuade the "yes" person. They become your bargaining allies.

One reason the "Conduit" technique is so effective is that it takes advantage of a powerful bargaining weapon—repetition. When you face the "yes" person's colleagues, you repeat your arguments—but not word for word. You take a fresh approach, pointing out other benefits and possibilities of your proposal.

Another reason the "Conduit" technique is so powerful is that the "yes" person isn't influenced directly by you. She is influenced by her trusted colleagues and co-workers, who have bought into your proposals. She is more likely to listen to them than to you.

I once negotiated with five opponents. I wasn't getting through to the "yes" person, so I focused on convincing the other four. As I kept speaking, I noticed one opponent begin nodding her approval. That improved my odds from 5 against 1 to 4 against 2. I kept on talking, and eventually 3 of the were 4 on my side. At that point the "yes" person was convinced as well.

The "Talk-Show Host" Technique

This technique is one of my favorites. You can get water from a rock using it. It gives you a way to approach delicate or touchy matters without offending your opponent.

Talk-show hosts use this technique all the time when they want to get some scandalous personal information from a guest. They'll say: "I don't want to get too personal, but..." or "I don't mean to pry, but..."

The "Talk-Show Host" technique hinges on four key words: *but, however, nevertheless,* and *except*. When a question is phrased using one or more of those words, it's nearly impossible to turn down. Next thing you know, the guest is admitting that he truly *is* the son of three-headed aliens with serious personality disorders.

This technique is very useful when you negotiate with family or friends. Say your son is asking for the car again, but he hasn't done his homework. That's against house rules, so you have to turn him down.

You can just say "no," but that's a sure way to send him stomping off to his room to sulk behind a closed door. Better to approach it like this: "I know how much you want to go out tonight. You know I always let you have the car after you've finished your homework, but..." This is a much sweeter pill to swallow, because you're acknowledging that a) the car means a lot to your son, and b) you'd let him have the car, if only he'd keep his end of the bargain. Deep down, your son will know you're right (even though he won't admit it).

The "Self-Deprecating" Technique

Self-deprecating statements break down barriers between you and your opponent. They make your opponent "like" you. They persuade your opponent without your opponent knowing it.

When you present a proposal to your opponent and think you might meet with some resistance, try a little self-deprecation. Suppose your child is having problems at school and you are asked to speak with the principal. As you check out the pictures in the principal's office, you discover that she is a parent, too. So you open the discussion by admitting how difficult parenting is. The principal will immediately relate to what you said. She will also be more sympathetic toward you, your problem, and any solutions you can suggest.

The "It's a Shame" Technique

When you're negotiating more than one issue, and a few issues have already been settled, you have an opportunity to use the "It's a Shame" technique.

Dealmaking Tip
The "It's a Shame" technique promotes successful negotiation by using easy, hard-to-disagree-with language. Avoid language that paints you into a corner, such as "I never," "I won't," or "I can't." If you make such a dramatic statement and later have to take it back, you will look weak in the eyes of your opponent.

It's a simple one. You've hit a stalemate on a few sticking points in your negotiation. You break the impasse by saying, "Look, we've taken care of so much. *It's a shame* to make that much progress without settling the remaining two issues. Let's give it a shot." Most of the time your opponent will go along. If you reach an agreement on the fifth issue and your opponent again resists, just repeat the "It's a Shame" technique.

"It's a Shame" is merely the name given to the technique. You can use a variety of phrases, such as "It's too bad that…" or "It's unfortunate that…" or "We've come this far, let's try to…" The point is, by using a key phrase, you use the already-agreed-upon issues as a basis for motivating your opponent to continue bargaining on the unresolved issues.

The Least You Need to Know

➤ As you prepare to negotiate, you should consider which negotiating techniques will work in your negotiation.

➤ Use the "Building Block" technique to impress your opponent with your knowledge and preparation.

➤ The "Vinegar and Honey" technique works by making a bad negotiating situation or concession seem better than it really is.

➤ The "Exhausting" and "Gear-Shifting" techniques work best on large, complex negotiations.

➤ Use the "Conduit" technique when you are facing more than one opponent and can't convince the "yes" person directly.

➤ The "Talk-Show Host" and "Self-Deprecating" techniques work to form a bond with your opponent.

➤ The "It's a Shame" technique works when a negotiation is nearly settled and only a few points remain to be discussed.

Part 3
You and Your Opponent

In the final analysis, successful negotiation means influencing your opponent's mind—his or her way of thinking—to agree to your bargaining positions. So the more you know about how the mind works, the more effective a negotiator you'll be.

As you gain bargaining experience, you'll see how easy it is to read your opponent's mind and how to use that knowledge to bargain successfully. In this part, I show you how to do it.

Chapter 11

The Types of Negotiating Opponents

In This Chapter

➤ Recognizing the best way to influence your opponent

➤ Determining how your opponent makes decisions

➤ Learning the best ways to negotiate with each type of opponent

In negotiation, as in life, you will face all kinds of people—people whose skills and talents lie in very different directions. Some can patiently plod through lists of figures, integrating complex statistics into one cogent analysis; others have a distinctive visual flair, a keen eye for color, shape, and design; still others are keen judges of character, capable of "reading" the new people they meet rapidly and with surprising accuracy.

If you can figure out which skills and preferences your opponent brings to the negotiating table, you can form a strategy that's best suited to persuading your opponent to give you what you want.

In this chapter, you learn about the different types of negotiating opponents and how to best influence each one.

What Are Your Influences?

While it's impossible to pigeonhole all people into one of three neat categories, you can get a rough idea of what type of information your opponent values most highly. Over the following pages, I categorize people into three broad "types"—*analytical*, *aesthetic*, and *intuitive*—in terms of the ways they are most strongly influenced. These "types" can be used as a rough psychological shorthand to help you size up your opponent and determine a negotiating strategy.

If you already researched your opponent (back in Chapter 3), you may want to review that research as you read this chapter. See if any of the information you've dug up clues you in to which "type" of opponent you face.

The Analytical Type

This type of person is most profoundly influenced by all things financial, statistical, and factual. She likes to be fully prepared before she enters into any discussion or negotiation; she wants "all the facts" before she makes a decision.

An analytical type is capable of making decisions she may not agree with personally if the numbers bear it out; for example, she might buy a house she isn't crazy about if it promises a good investment opportunity. On the job, she might roll out a new product that she wouldn't buy personally if the marketing research suggests that it will be an instant best-seller.

> **Dealmaking Tip**
> Practice distinguishing "types" with all the people you come into contact with. When you're bargaining it will be easier for you to figure out which type your opponent is.

Analytical types can be found, not surprisingly, in occupations that require a head for figures: accountants, financial analysts, business managers, chief financial officers, and tax consultants. Frequently, corporate presidents and business owners also have an analytical side because they are constantly asked to analyze profit and loss statements, expenses, budgets, and so on.

Here are some signs that you're bargaining with an analytical type:

➤ She immediately asks for hard facts, such as sales figures, price, profit potential, financing options, or fees.

➤ He is interested in the financial history of the product or service you are negotiating for. How well did the widgets sell in the past? How much of a return did you make on the investment property? How much of a raise did you receive last year? These figures will give him a sense of the future potential of the deal.

➤ She asks to see documentation (sales figures, reports, receipts) of your assertions.

Here are some hints to help you influence an analytical type:

➤ Be fully primed and prepared with any information related to the financial or factual side of the deal. For example, if you're bargaining to sell your home, have figures on the cost, price you paid for the house, the cost of the repair work you've done, the taxes you pay, and so on, down cold.

➤ Downplay aesthetic or intuitive arguments, such as how nice your house looks, or how what a good neighborhood it's in. The analytical opponent wants the hard facts first.

➤ The more you can document on paper (such as sales graphs, receipts, or cost estimates), the more you will influence the analytical type.

The Aesthetic Type

The aesthetic type focuses on how things look and feel, and what kind of visceral impact they have. He may be openly dismissive or scornful of facts and figures in favor of more artistic considerations. In terms of selling your home, for example, an aesthetic type might actually pay more for your house (if he really likes the way it looks) than an analytical type.

Many artists, writers, actors, designers, and other people who work in creative occupations tend to be aesthetic types.

Here are some signs that you're bargaining with an aesthetic type:

➤ He places great importance on the way things look. For example, if you're showing him your home, he may become wide-eyed as he views your beautifully landscaped lawn. On the other hand, nothing turns him off so quickly as an unkempt or dirty room or yard.

➤ She is quick to point out sights (and even smells and sounds) that she likes or dislikes.

➤ Aesthetic types may also be more tactile than other types: they often like to touch objects (run a hand over a countertop, feel a piece of drapery or fabric, and so on).

Here are some hints to help you influence an aesthetic type:

➤ Emphasize the appearance, condition, and quality of the product or service you are negotiating for. Make sure the product or service has spectacular "eye appeal."

➤ Beyond the obvious appearance of whatever you are negotiating for, emphasize subtle but important aesthetic concerns. For example, if you are showing your house, point out the flow of the floor design or the play of light and shade from the windows.

The Intuitive Type

The intuitive type is influenced by one major consideration—how he "feels" about what you're bargaining about. If his "gut" feeling about you or the negotiation is good, he'll be happy to work with you. If he doesn't "have a good feeling," on the other hand, you'll have to work extra hard to overcome his bad impression and seal the deal.

Intuitive types tend to make decisions very quickly. Oftentimes, if pressed for an explanation, they can't even verbalize why they make the decisions they do. That's because they operate primarily on instinct.

People who work in jobs that require rapid analysis, diagnosis, and action, such as doctors, lawyers, and salespeople, are often the intuitive type. Lawyers, for example, often spend a lot of time analyzing a client's problems and then must make on-the-spot decisions when they try the case in front of a jury.

Here are some signs that you are bargaining with an intuitive type:

➤ He gives you plenty of verbal and physical feedback to show what he thinks of your proposal. If he likes what he's seeing and hearing, he may nod frequently and say "Uh-huh" or "I see." If he doesn't like what you're saying, he may frown, shake his head, or express his displeasure in some other way.

➤ She may make quick, generalized snap judgments: "I don't like it. It doesn't feel right." Or: "I have a good feeling about this. I think it's going to work out."

Intuitive types can be tricky to negotiate with, because if they simply don't like you, you will be hard-pressed to win them over. But here are some hints to help you influence an intuitive type:

➤ Be especially careful to cultivate a bond with this type. (See Chapter 14 for advice on building up goodwill with your opponent.) While you should do this with all negotiating opponents, intuitive types place especially strong emphasis on trusting and liking the people they negotiate with.

➤ Emphasize how well the deal will suit both of you. Intuitive types are keen to act on negotiations that feel right and that are fair to everyone involved in them.

A Word of Caution About Types

It's impossible to boil down a person of myriad experiences, emotions, and preferences into a single "type." For one thing, many people may straddle one or more types. A marketing manager, for example, may be equally concerned with the aesthetics of a product design and the financial analysis of how well the product will sell. A salesperson, on the other hand, may operate on both intuitive and analytical levels as she tries to clinch a sale.

In addition, as you prepare for a negotiation, you should be well-versed in arguments that will convince all three "types." Don't assume, for example, that because you are negotiating with an aesthetic type, you can ignore or fudge the financial aspect of your negotiation. That's unrealistic and insulting to your opponent.

So use these "types" as a rough guideline, not the final word on your opponent's psyche.

How Your Opponent Makes Decisions: The Strong-Weak Continuum

There's another refinement you can use as you try to size up your opponent. In addition to discovering the way your opponent is most strongly influenced, you can quickly determine *how* she makes decisions.

Whether your opponent is primarily analytical, aesthetic, or intuitive, she also operates on a continuum of decision-making, from strong to weak. An aesthetic type who is a strong decision-maker, for example, probably has highly developed views on what looks good and what does not; she has a strong design sense. An aesthetic type who is a weak decision-maker, on the other hand, may have less firmly set views.

Just as the analytical-aesthetic-intuitive labels are guidelines, not final judgments, so is the strong-weak continuum. Most negotiators will fall somewhere in the middle. Use this as a general guideline to determine how best to negotiate with your opponent.

The Strong (Not-So-Silent) Type

Whether they operate primarily on analytical, aesthetic, or intuitive levels, strong types make decisions quickly and confidently. They analyze complicated information rapidly—but sometimes, when they pass judgment too quickly, their hasty decisions turn out to be wrong.

If you're trying to sell your home to a strong type, for example, she will go after your property aggressively if she really loves it. She may want to rush the deal through without bargaining—even if it means she has to pay a higher price for your place.

Most strong types display some or all of the following traits:

➤ They interrupt frequently and often answer your questions before you've finished asking them.

➤ They use "I" a lot because they have a strong desire for recognition.

➤ Their speak in a firm, unhesitant tone of voice. They always talk and act like they know what they're doing—even if they secretly have doubts.

➤ They get angry quickly and take a long time to calm down.

Negotiating With a Strong Type

While strong types seem commanding and authoritative, they're easy to deal with if you use the following strategies:

➤ Strong types respond best to clear, logical positions that leave no unanswered questions or areas open to interpretation. So if you're negotiating with a strong type, present your proposals clearly and back them up with as much documentation as you can.

Take that house you're selling. The strong type is likely to give you the price you're asking for without question if you've got a written appraisal that proves the house is worth it.

➤ Strong types tend to stick to their views or judgments, even after they've been proven wrong (which, incidentally, doesn't happen often). That's because it's excruciating for these types to admit that they've made a mistake. (Sound familiar?)

If you catch a strong type making a mistake, you can gain the negotiating edge by pointing out the error. (Just be tactful—don't gloat.) Most strong types have a definite sense of right and wrong, and if you point out an error they will usually make concessions— sometimes large ones—to "put things right."

Dealmaking Tip
Once you've figured out the type of opponent you're negotiating with, don't let on that you have your opponent pegged. Continue to act as you always have—while you inwardly develop your strategies to fit the type of person you're dealing with.

➤ Strong types get angry quickly, and they stay angry. So don't do or say anything that will set them off.

One of the easiest ways to make strong types angry is by not taking them seriously. If you have to reject a strong type's offer, you should explain in detail why you're turning him down. And never laugh at or belittle a proposal made by a strong type, no matter how off-the-wall it seems.

The Fence-Straddling Type

Unlike the strong type, who will have immediate and decisive views on any issue or negotiation, the fence-straddling type needs more time and likes to reach a consensus before taking any action. Here are some clues to help you spot this type:

> ➤ Fence-straddling types like to feel that they've exhausted all possible approaches before they make a final decision. They hoard all paperwork related to the issue, and they tend to consult with others (colleagues, family, friends, experts) to get a wide variety of opinions.

> ➤ They will usually ask for time to consult with others before they make a final decision on any major proposals, but they are quick to concede minor points.

It's Been Said
"Indecision is debilitating; it feeds upon itself; it is, one might almost say, habit-forming...often greater risk is involved in postponement than in making the wrong decision."
—H.A. Hopt

Negotiating With a Fence-Straddling Type

Here's how you can break through the fence-straddler's indecision:

> ➤ When a fence-straddler leaves a negotiation to consult with others, he often comes back to the bargaining table with all kinds of changes and variations. Don't let him get away! Explain your proposals to him in great detail and try to "force" him to make a decision on the spot.

> ➤ If other people whose opinions are important to your opponent agree with your negotiating position, you should mention this to the fence-straddling type, who likes to reach consensus. For example, you might say, "I've heard that your business manager thinks that 50 cents a widget will work with your budget."

The Weak Type

Weak types, whether analytical, aesthetic, or intuitive, make for unfortunate negotiators. They are reluctant to make any decisions—they would much rather pass the responsibility on to family members, business associates, or friends. They stall, they stammer, they beg for more information and more time. They try to postpone any decision until it's forced upon them.

Here are some other clues to help you spot weak types:

➤ They tend to be timid and speak quietly. They let you do all the talking and only occasionally offer a nod or an "Uh-huh." They almost never interrupt.

➤ Because decision making is nerve-wracking for them, they are prone to bad habits such as nail-biting and squinting.

Negotiating With a Weak Type

If you apply too much pressure on weak types, they will simply abdicate the decision to someone else. Instead, be very patient. Explain every major proposal you make in detail. Encourage them to ask questions so they can participate in the bargaining process. That's often the only way you'll make progress.

The Least You Need to Know

➤ Try to figure out as early as possible whether your opponent is an analytical, aesthetic, or intuitive type.

➤ Analytical types are most influenced by figures, statistics, and hard data.

➤ Aesthetic types are most influenced by things that look, feel, taste, smell, and sound good to them. Cultivate a lot of "eye appeal" when you negotiate with these types.

➤ Intuitive types often operate on gut feeling and instinct. Concentrate on developing a bond with them before you negotiate.

➤ If you are negotiating with a strong type, take her proposals seriously and provide a lot of documentation for your proposals.

➤ If you are negotiating with a fence-straddling type, press him to make a decision without consulting with others.

➤ If you are negotiating with a weak type, be patient and explain every detail of your proposal.

Chapter 12

Appealing to Your Opponent's Self

In This Chapter

➤ Why it's important to know how to reach your opponent's self

➤ Appealing to your opponent's self to promote your position

➤ Making sure your opponent is not appealing to your self

Shortly after she moved to a new neighborhood, Sally visited the local diner for breakfast. She wasn't crazy about the food and she thought the service was poor. The next day, she mentioned how bad the place was to her neighbor.

A few weeks later, Sally revisited the diner. This time, the owner came out to greet her personally. He served her himself and made sure everything was perfect.

Sally reported the welcome change to her neighbor. "I wonder what happened? Did you tell the owner about my complaints?" she asked.

"Actually," her neighbor said, "I told him you were very impressed with his service and said that was how he must have built up such a good business."

The lesson here? You will always get more out of people if you compliment rather than criticize them. We negotiators call this appealing to your opponent's *self*. In this chapter, you learn how to recognize—and appeal to—the essential parts of your opponent's self.

Your "Self"—All You Consider to Be Yours

Quick—describe your "self."

Difficult, isn't it? That's because there are so many different facets of your "self." You are defined, in part, by the people you associate with—your family, friends, employer, and co-workers. They're a part of your "self." So are the things you own: your clothes, house, money, and car. The intangibles, like your reputation and values, are part of you too. Literally everything you are connected to is part of your identity.

It's Been Said

"Neither threats nor pleading can move a man unless they touch some one of his potential or actual selves. Only thus can we, as a rule, get a purchase on another's will. The first care of diplomatists and monarchs and all who wish to rule or influence is, accordingly, to find out their victim's strongest principle of self-regard, so as to make that the fulcrum of all appeals."
—William James

You are emotionally attached to all of these things, but not with the same intensity. You're more strongly attached to your family, for example, than to your neighbor or your car. (I hope.) So your degree of attachment depends on how closely you consider anything to be part of your self.

If you have children, think about how fiercely protective you are of them. When anyone criticizes them, you immediately rise to defend them—not just because of the criticism, but because in your mind, when someone attacks your children, it feels like that person is attacking you. Likewise, when your kids do well, you glow with pride—not just for them, but for yourself. Your kids are that much a part of you. Whatever happens to them touches your self.

If you can discover what is an important part of your opponent's self, you can establish a bond with your opponent—and this will make negotiating easier, more fruitful, and more enjoyable for both of you.

Discovering What Turns Your Opponent On

Back in Chapter 3, I talked about how important it is to research your opponent before you begin negotiating. During your research, try to discover some of your opponent's interests and values. Better still, look for those interests and values that you and your opponent have in common.

See if you can find any mention of your opponent's:

➤ Professional achievements

➤ Family life

➤ Artistic pursuits

➤ Athletic ability

➤ Intellectual accomplishments

➤ Volunteer work

➤ Hobbies

If you can't discover anything beforehand, you'll only have a few minutes before negotiating begins to look for tip-offs to your opponent's personality. Look around his office, if that's where you are. (Of course, you'll try *not* to be there, because that's his home field.) Study any plaques on the wall, books on the shelf, or pictures or nicknacks on the desk. If your opponent has come to you, make a quick study of his physical appearance for clues (but don't stare).

The initial conversation you make with your opponent before negotiation begins can also offer you a wealth of chances to learn more about her. Ask questions about her business, her schooling, or even her hobbies if you feel it's appropriate.

Do it tactfully and sincerely. You don't want your opponent to think that you're snooping into areas that are none of your business. But most people like to talk about themselves and will tell you a lot about themselves without hesitation.

The sooner and more you can learn, the better. You want as much time as possible to use what you've learned during the bargaining.

Why Appeal to Your Opponent's Self?

You have three objectives when you appeal to your opponent's self:

➤ You want to create a more compatible relationship with your opponent *as a person.*

➤ You want to form a bond between the two of you.

➤ You want to know the best way to influence and persuade your opponent.

Difficult though it may be, you have to separate the issue that you are negotiating from the person you are negotiating with. Even if the negotiation is controversial and the discussions become intense, you still have to treat your opponent as a person.

You can be a tough-as-nails negotiator—but a respectful, courteous, and patient person. That's the only way you'll ever reach your opponent's self. Once that cardinal rule is forgotten, and negotiating breaks down, cases end up in court, unions go on strike, and friends become enemies.

Negotiating is much easier once you and your opponent have a bond, like belonging to the same organization. Having a bond makes you a part of your opponent's self.

When I'm negotiating with a lawyer, for example, I always check his background to see if we have anything in common (such as belonging to the same legal fraternity). If I find something, I mention it as early in the bargaining as possible. That makes me a part of my opponent's self and he a part of my self.

How to Appeal to Your Opponent's Self

Say your daughter is having a problem with one of her teachers at school, and you have to talk to the principal about it. You've read in the last PTA bulletin that the principal recently received an award for outstanding school administrator. You can assume the principal's very proud of that award. It represents her accomplishments and all she's worked so hard for so many difficult years. It's a part of her self.

When you sit down to speak with the principal, you open with a compliment: "You know, I'm so happy that Margie's enrolled in this school. The classes and activities are great. And congratulations on winning the Outstanding School Administrator award! You must be really proud." That does the trick. You've touched your opponent's self. Now you're both relaxed and you can move into your discussion in an atmosphere of mutual cooperation and agreement.

Dealmaking Tip

Most people realize that flattery stems from some degree of self-interest on the part of the flatterer—but for some reason, in most cases flattery still works anyway. Only when your flattery is clearly insincere will you have problems.

Or, say your opponent mentions that she belongs to the same charitable group as you—you both volunteer for the Salvation Army during the holidays to help raise money. Talking about your mutual interest will appeal to your opponent's self and will form a bond between you that will make your negotiation proceed more smoothly.

A lot of times your opponent may be fishing—even hoping—for a compliment. Stay alert and you'll be able to pick up the clues. If your opponent is vain about his appearance, for example, he may make unconscious gestures like smoothing down his tie or brushing imaginary lint off his suit. If you sense that a compliment is in order, go for it. Tell your opponent what a great suit he has on. You'll see an immediate reaction. Your opponent will warm up to you. You've hit him where he's most responsive—his self.

Dealbreaker Alert

Always make your compliments sincere. Your opponent will be insulted if he detects or even suspects that you're faking it.

Open Mouth, Insert Foot—Offending Your Opponent's Self

You're flustered. You're late to meet with your opponent because your plane was delayed. You show up at his office and say, "Sorry, but the terminal was a zoo, none of the attendants knew what was going on, and I ended up sitting on an unmoving plane for over an hour before we got cleared for takeoff. You know how those damned airlines are."

Your opponent frowns and says, "Yes, actually I do. My father, brother, and sister are commercial pilots."

Oops! Anything can happen once you make the mistake of offending your opponent's self. Your opponent may seethe quietly, or tell you off. Whatever the reaction, one thing is certain: negotiating with this person won't be easy.

Say your opponent casually says she and her family just returned from a fabulous two-week camping trip. If you hate the outdoors and just the thought of camping makes you itchy, keep it to yourself. Say something neutral like, "That's great. Sounds like a lot of fun." You've kept your comments positive and, more importantly, you didn't injure your opponent's self.

Some subjects to avoid so you don't attack your opponent's self:

➤ Negative opinions or gossip about your opponent's company, product, or colleagues

➤ Negative opinions on hobbies, movies, books, or interests—unless you know for sure your opponent agrees

➤ Jokes (unless you know your opponent's sense of humor well)

➤ Anything to do with religion or politics

Of course, you're only human and there will be times when you unintentionally offend your opponent. What do you do if that happens? Simple: Apologize! Right there, on the spot. If you wait too long to apologize, your opponent may think you're insincere—and then you're a goner.

Don't Get Offended—Handling Assaults on Your Self

I once negotiated with an opponent who opened the discussions by accusing me of insulting his intelligence. I was negotiating to buy his property—a golf course he had helped to design—and I mentioned that my client needed to make changes on the property. I was trying to get the purchase price lowered to cover the cost of the changes.

My opponent was so personally attached to the course and the design that he attacked me for suggesting that anything should be done to change it. I stayed cool, smiled, and then carefully explained that nothing personal was intended by the suggested changes. The issue was return on our investment and the changes were proposed solely for economic reasons—not to personally offend him. That did the trick. He calmed down and we resumed bargaining.

It's Been Said

"One cool judgment is worth a thousand hasty councils."
—Woodrow Wilson

Your goal is to learn to be thick-skinned when you negotiate. (I know, I know, it's a lot easier said than done.) You'll bargain with a lot of opponents who may offend you, either because they lack experience or are just mean-spirited. Keep your eye on the issues, not the people involved. In Chapter 20 I'll talk more about what to do if personality conflicts get really out of hand.

Don't Let Your Opponent Appeal to Your Self

While you are saying nice things about your opponent's professional expertise, beautiful family, or well-tended widget collection, your opponent will be equally quick to stroke you about your accomplishments, your family, and your interests. You know she's trying to appeal to your self. What do you do?

Be gracious. Thank your opponent. Then move on with the discussion as quickly as possible. Don't dwell on your opponent's remarks. (Another piece of advice that's easier said than done.) If you dwell on your opponent's remarks, you're increasing the chances that they will influence you to make concessions.

We all like people who stroke us and build up our ego. But don't let a little flattery persuade you to make concessions that work against your interests. That's a high price to pay for a little buttering up.

The Least You Need to Know

➤ Learn as much as you can about your opponent before negotiation so you know what will best appeal to your opponent's self.

➤ Appealing to your opponent's self creates a closer relationship, which makes your opponent more likely to give you what you want.

➤ Sincere compliments will appeal to your opponent's self. So will finding that you share something in common, such as belonging to the same club or working for the same charity.

➤ Never offer insincere compliments.

➤ Never be critical of anything that's not relevant to the bargaining because you may unintentionally offend your opponent's self.

➤ If you offend your opponent's self, apologize.

➤ Don't make any concessions because your opponent has appealed to your self. Focus on getting what you want.

WELL, I GUESS I COULD CONCEDE THAT POINT...

Chapter 13

Appealing to Your Opponent's Emotions

In This Chapter

➤ Why you should appeal to your opponent's emotions

➤ The three factors that will strongly influence your opponent's emotions

➤ How to use those elements when you negotiate

Every one of us is a bundle of emotions. Fear, anger, grief, joy, rage, and shame, to name only a few, lay quietly within us, waiting for the right stimulant to wake up.

Playing on the emotions is an age-old practice—a trade that politicians, playwrights, and poets, among others, have been plying for centuries. Negotiators do, too. In this chapter, I show you how to recognize what triggers your opponent's emotions and then use that knowledge to influence the negotiation.

It's Been Said
"Emotions come wholly from within, and have only the strength we allow them. Emotions are the color of life; we would be drab creatures without them. But we must control those emotions or they will control us."
—John M. Wilson

Why Should You Play the Emotional Angle?

When you're emotionally involved in something, you don't look at it objectively and impartially. You substitute your emotional judgment for a judgment based on the merits of a position. Appealing to your opponent's emotions is thus a separate form of persuasion from trying to persuade your opponent on the merits of your bargaining position.

It's Been Said
"There is a road from the eye to the heart that does not go through the intellect."
—G.K. Chesterton

Therein lies its real worth. If your bargaining position is weak on merit, you can appeal to your opponent's emotions. You want to get your opponent to forget about your weak negotiating position and be emotionally motivated to give you what you want.

Three Ways to Make Your Opponent Emotional

It's Been Said
"When dealing with people, remember you are not dealing with creatures of logic, but with creatures of emotion."
—Dale Carnegie

There are many ways to influence your opponent's emotions. In negotiation, the three most direct routes to emotional influence are:

➤ Wealth

➤ Recognition

➤ Self-preservation

In each of the following sections, we look at the different emotional influences and how they can affect negotiation.

Give Me Money (That's What I Want)

For many of us, a part of the great American dream is to get rich. We all have a strong desire for wealth, which includes money, property, valuables, or anything else that we attach value to. Wealth gives us power, freedom, and security (not to mention the ability to take off for Bora Bora whenever we feel like it). Most of us have a strong desire to accumulate more wealth and protect what we have.

Many of your opponents will have a strong desire for wealth. So if your bargaining strategy is to cut a deal that will either increase their wealth or help them to preserve their existing wealth, you'll strike their emotional nerve.

Here's how to recognize opponents with a strong craving for wealth:

➤ They like to talk about and show off their possessions: expensive car, house, clothes, and so on.

➤ They often like to talk about anything that relates to money, such as the killing they made in the stock market or their company profits.

➤ Expressions dealing with money—"bucks," "big ones," "moola," "greenbacks," etc.—often pop up in their conversation.

➤ They frequently talk about other people's money with a hint of envy.

➤ They tend to have a negative, almost condescending attitude toward people who don't have a lot of money.

I Love the Spotlight—Recognition

People have a strong desire to be recognized and acknowledged for their achievements. A skillful actress wants her fans and colleagues to notice and admire her technique. A high-powered businessman wants others to pay tribute to his flamboyant wheeling and dealing. An all-star athlete wants to win medals for her athletic prowess.

Here's how to recognize opponents with a strong craving for recognition:

➤ They're often driven to get themselves and their accomplishments splashed across any media that will have them, whether it's a local newspaper, magazine, television, or even word of mouth.

➤ They are usually well-groomed, and may wear flashy clothes.

➤ Their material goods are usually impeccable—they have well-tended homes and cars (often with custom license plates).

➤ They may refer to themselves frequently in conversation; their favorite words are "I" or "me."

➤ They often work in the public eye (actors, politicians, athletes, executives, celebrities).

➤ They often work in uniform (military officers, airline pilots, police).

Gimme Shelter—Self-Preservation

Self-preservation is the desire to be physically and financially safe and secure. Anything that ensures or threatens that security will get an emotional response. If someone sticks a gun in your face and tells you to do something, you'll do it because you value your life. If someone threatens your job, you'd have the same self-preservation reaction, but to a less extreme degree.

Self-preservation will be the strongest desire of many of your opponents. We all want to be safe and secure, but some people take that desire to extremes. They squirrel away every dime, even though they have enough money to last a lifetime. They obey the speed limit, cross only at the intersection, and observe every rule and regulation because it gives them a feeling of safety.

Dealmaking Tip

Try to discover what will emotionally motivate your opponent while you're bargaining. Is it wealth? Recognition? Self-preservation? Once you learn which is the strongest motivator, you can develop a strategy to appeal to it, especially if the merits of your bargaining position are weak.

Here's how to recognize opponents with a strong craving for self-preservation:

➤ Generally, they are not aggressive. They are good listeners who will let you talk, because they feel more secure when they know what's on your mind.

➤ They are usually low-key. They don't get excited or angry easily.

➤ They dress plainly, since they don't crave recognition for their appearance or their financial status.

How to Appeal to Your Opponent's Emotions

Once you know which emotional appeal is strongest for your opponent—wealth, recognition, or self-preservation—you have an additional weapon in your negotiating arsenal. It gives you more bargaining flexibility.

Offering Your Opponent Money

Any of your bargaining positions that increase or preserve your opponent's wealth will prompt an emotional response. The more your opponent wants wealth, the quicker and stronger your opponent's emotional response will be.

For example, I once had a job collecting debts for a car dealership. I sent a simple letter to the debtors, promising that if they didn't pay, the dealership would take "appropriate action" which would cause them "additional expenses." Aside from using fear as a motivator (which I'll discuss in Chapter 19), I was really advising them that they could preserve their wealth if they promptly paid off their debt. I was appealing to their desire for wealth.

Dealmaking Tip

Your opponent's strong desire for wealth is a fruitful area of emotional appeal. Whenever you can demonstrate that your proposals will increase or preserve your opponent's wealth, you've got a sound bargaining strategy.

If I would have offered them a ten-percent discount for paying promptly, I would have also been appealing to preserving their wealth. It would be the same if I offered a $100 gift certificate because they would have been $100 richer.

To give one more example, say you're selling your home, which has an additional acre attached that's worth $10,000. You've just about persuaded the buyer to pay full price for your house, but he hasn't signed on the dotted line. So you throw in a sweet-ener—the right to buy the attached lot for $8,000, any time within three years from the date you sell your home. If your opponent's strong desire is wealth, he will emotionally respond to the opportunity to get a good deal on the attached property.

It's Been Said
"The acquisition of wealth is a work of great labor; its possession, a source of continued fear; its loss, a source of excessive grief." —Latin saying

Offering Your Opponent Recognition

If your opponent craves recognition, he will be receptive to any deal that will increase his visibility. And if his desire for recognition is strong enough, the money part of the deal becomes secondary. Anything you do that appeals to his desire for recognition will emotionally motivate him.

Dealbreaker Alert

When you're appealing to your opponent's emotions, give in on minor concessions. You don't want to get bogged down in petty disputes and run the risk of angering your opponent. If you do, your opponent will not respond to your emotional appeals.

For example, during one negotiation I suggested to my opponent that if we reached an agreement, we should hold a press conference to announce it. I knew he had a strong desire for recognition and would shine in front of the camera. Slipping the press conference suggestion into the negotiation emotionally stimulated my opponent to reach an agreement.

Or say you're bargaining with a landscaper to redo the design of the shrubbery and flowers around your front lawn. You promise the landscaper that you will leave her sign on your property for 30 days after the job is completed, so everyone who passes by your house will know that Smith Landscaping did the job. Not only does this promise good business for Smith, but it also directly appeals to her desire for recognition for a landscaping job well done.

Offering Your Opponent Security

Anything you say or do that preserves and ensures your opponent's self-preservation will cause him to emotionally respond.

For example, say you own a beautiful and intricate grandfather clock, passed down from your grandparents to your parents and now to you. You intend to pass the clock on to your own children someday. But time has taken its toll (bad pun!) and the delicate clock mechanism needs repairs. A specialist examines the clock and estimates that a full repair will cost nearly $1,000.

You don't really have that kind of money. But you do have a strong desire for self-preservation. The repair person senses this and clinches it by suggesting that the clock mechanism will completely break if you don't take action soon.

Your urge to preserve the clock will be very strong because it's a part of your family and a part of your "self." You'll probably fork up the money because you want to preserve the things that are close and dear to you. By preserving those things, you're preserving a part of your self.

The Least You Need to Know

➤ When your negotiating position is weak on its merits, you should consider appealing to your opponent's emotions to get what you want.

➤ All people have a desire for wealth, recognition, and self-preservation.

➤ You should determine which of the three desires most strongly motivates your opponent and appeal to that desire when you negotiate.

Using Goodwill (the Concept, not the Charity)

Earlier in my career, when I worked with the Treasury Department in Chicago, I was constantly called upon to negotiate with high-powered lawyers who represented the estates of wealthy decedents.

In one case, a lawyer didn't want to include a particular asset in his late client's estate. That would raise the estate taxes. But I knew of a tax loophole that would offset the added tax, and I told him about it. We concluded our business successfully and cordially. He later called me to thank me again for letting him in on that inside information.

By doing my opponent that small but significant favor, I built up goodwill with him. In this chapter, you learn what goodwill is and how you can harness its powers in your negotiations.

Why It's Necessary to Build Goodwill

Goodwill simply means doing your opponent a favor, just as I did when I pointed out that tax reduction to the estate lawyer. When you build goodwill with your opponent, what you're really doing is developing a relationship of mutual trust and compatibility.

Let's Talk Terms
Goodwill is defined by *Webster's New World Dictionary* as "benevolence; willingness; the value of a business as a result of patronage, reputation, etc.; beyond its tangible assets."

That kind of bargaining environment is the one in which both you and your opponent are most likely to seal a successful deal. Your opponent will concede points and issues he normally wouldn't dream of giving in on, solely because he has a favorable perception of you.

There are innumerable political, social, and psychological benefits of doing good things for others. But in strictly negotiating terms, there are four specific reasons why you should build goodwill:

➤ It serves as a bridge of trust between you and your opponent. Once your opponent trusts you, it will be easier to persuade her. She will accept your words, assertions, and any written material you offer. Then you are practicing the art of persuasion at its finest. You're reaching and influencing your opponent.

➤ Goodwill ensures that your opponent will like you. I admit, likeability doesn't sound like a quality tough negotiators should boast about—but it is. If your opponent likes you, he'll be more likely to give you what you want.

➤ If you build goodwill with your opponent the first time the two of you negotiate, you'll have an easy time whenever you negotiate again.

➤ Once you build goodwill with an opponent, he will tell others how pleasant it was to work with you. It's basic human nature to talk about people we like—and dislike.

It's Been Said
"The ability...to make people believe in you and trust you is one of the few absolutely fundamental qualities of success."
—John J. McGuirk

If your opponent is a goodwill ambassador for you, sooner or later, the benefits will surface. I frequently negotiate with new opponents who tell me they feel comfortable with me solely because of what they've heard about me from my previous opponents. That's in spite of the fact that I have a reputation as a tough, tenacious negotiator.

Dealmaking Tip

People who like each other tend to reach agreements fast. People who don't, won't.

How Can You Build Goodwill?

There are many ways you can build a bridge of goodwill to your opponent:

➤ *Tip off your client to any hidden benefits in your proposal.* That's what I did when I informed that estate lawyer about the tax benefits he wasn't aware of. That's one of the best ways to get your opponent in the right frame of mind. Each favor you do for your opponent builds a plank in the bridge of trust...even if you're hard-hitting at the bargaining table.

➤ *Point out* any *errors your opponent makes, as early in the negotiations as possible and as tactfully as possible.* Your opponent will owe you a big favor when you help save his face in a negotiation.

For example, I once negotiated with an opponent who mistook an asset valued at $750,000 for only $75,000. I quickly corrected him before he completely embarrassed himself and botched the deal. From that point on, he warmed up to me and was very receptive to my proposals.

Realize here that I'm referring to obvious errors that have an important impact on the negotiation. You don't have to monitor your opponent's entire case. But obvious errors will come to light, sooner or later. You can both head off problems and build up goodwill by pointing them out sooner.

Dealbreaker Alert

Always point out obvious errors immediately. If you wait too long, your opponent will suspect that you were trying to think of a way to benefit from the error. This will make your opponent suspicious of you, and a suspicious opponent is not one very likely to agree with your bargaining position.

➤ *Make suggestions that help your opponent if the bargaining is successfully concluded.* Back in Chapter 13, I mentioned a time when I did that by suggesting a press conference to an opponent to satisfy his strong desire for recognition.

When you negotiate a deal to buy something—clothes, a car, a new house—you can always promise good word-of-mouth to your opponent if you're happy with your purchase. That will make your opponent feel good about the deal and about you.

Think of any "extras" that you can throw in that will motivate your opponent to go along with your proposals and feel good once the deed is done.

➤ *Cultivate a personal touch.* This is where the research you've done on your opponent comes into play (see Chapter 3). Ask about your opponent's family, career, hobbies...whatever you can think of. Just make sure you're sincere. If you genuinely don't care or can't stand your opponent, don't try to "make nice."

➤ *Express your appreciation.* Anything you think will go over well with your opponent is something to do. Think of all the generous, dramatic gestures that companies make to woo important clients—tickets to sports and theater events, holiday gift baskets, celebratory bottles of champagne on completion of a project. You don't have to send your opponent to a sporting match or a Broadway show to earn goodwill—but a nice card acknowledging that you enjoyed meeting and working with your opponent wouldn't be a bad idea.

When Not to Give Goodwill: A Cautionary Note

In almost every instance, goodwill is an important asset in your negotiation. But there's one important exception: your attempts at goodwill must not harm your *bargaining position*. You don't have to reveal your negotiating strategy, point out any flaws in your argument, relinquish your terms, or compromise your own position simply to build goodwill with your opponent. Remember, it's not your job to help win your opponent's case.

It's Been Said
"Today's profits are yesterday's goodwill ripened."
—Eugene P. Berten

The Least You Need to Know

➤ Always try to build goodwill with your opponent. Goodwill builds trust, makes negotiation easier, and will build your reputation as a good negotiator.

➤ You can build goodwill by doing your opponent a favor, pointing out errors your opponent has made, agreeing to help promote your opponent's interests, showing concern for your opponent, or doing anything else that benefits your opponent.

➤ Anything you do to build up goodwill with your opponent should not harm your bargaining position.

Part 4
Increasing Your Negotiating Power

The word "power" means the ability to accomplish objectives. When you bargain, you have an objective. It may be to get back money, to buy something you want at a fair price, or to gain some peace of mind.

That's where power comes in. If you have negotiating power, your task of accomplishing your negotiating objectives will be much easier. In this part, I show you how increasing your negotiating power helps you get any of the things you decide to negotiate for.

I'VE GOT NEGOTIATING POWER!!

NEGOTIATOR

Chapter 15

Negotiating Power: How to Get It, How to Use It

In This Chapter

➤ Discovering your negotiating power

➤ Unleashing your negotiating power

➤ Keeping your opponent aware of your negotiating power

➤ How to use mental rehearsal to boost your negotiating power

The word "power" usually calls to mind physical strength or far-reaching financial or political influence. When you think of powerful people, you might picture Michael Jordan or the President of the United States.

Fortunately, negotiating power doesn't rely on a commanding presence or influential job (although both can be part of negotiating power). That's because when you bargain, you pit your mind against your opponent's mind. Your negotiating power palette includes all of your preparation for the negotiation, your knowledge of the subject matter and your opponent, and how you play out your bargaining hand.

The trick is to discover what power you have and how and when to use it. After you read this chapter, you'll know all about power and how to use it when you bargain.

What Is Negotiating Power?

Negotiating power is anything you can use to motivate your opponent to give you what you want. This broad definition includes:

➤ Your knowledge of the negotiating situation

➤ Your knowledge of what motivates your opponent

➤ The negotiating options open to you and the options open to your opponent—and how you play them out during the bargaining

➤ Your negotiating experience and how you use it

➤ Your reputation or your company's reputation

➤ All the bargaining techniques you have at your disposal (see Part 2)

As you answer the questions in the following Negotiating Power worksheet, you will be better able to pinpoint the exact sources of your negotiating power.

Negotiating Power Worksheet

1. What am I willing to offer my opponent in order to meet my goals?

   Money: _____

   Payment Schedule: _____

   Time: _____

   Service: _____

   Improvements: _____

   Returns: _____

   Future Business: _____

   Volume Deals: _____

   Other: _____

2. How badly does my opponent need what I am willing to offer?

   Money: _____

   Payment Schedule: _____

   Time: _____

Service: _____

Improvements: _____

Returns: _____

Future Business: _____

Volume Deals: _____

Other: _____

3. How can I appeal to my opponent's self as I negotiate?

    _____

4. How can I appeal to my opponent's emotions as I negotiate?

    _____

5. What is my negotiating reputation or the reputation of those associated with me? (broker, company, etc.)

    _____

6. How can I build up goodwill with my opponent?

    _____

7. What else do I have or can I do to motivate my opponent?

    _____

When you skillfully use your negotiating power, your opponent *will* be favorably motivated to reach an agreement. That's a certainty.

The Rules of the Game: Using Negotiating Power

There are a few basic rules when it comes to making your opponent aware of, and, if necessary, using, your negotiating power. In the following pages, I show you the different types of negotiating power and how you can use them.

As you bargain, remind yourself of the negotiating power you have so that if you have an opportunity to use it, you can.

First, distinguish between knowledge of power and use of power. Making your opponent aware of your power is different than actually using it.

Remember the Woody Allen movie *Take the Money and Run*? Woody's hapless character tries to rob a bank but gets nowhere because the teller misreads his note: "I have a gub." A small phalanx of bank representatives crowd around the teller and Woody—the would-be robber armed with a deadly weapon—watches helplessly as they all try to decipher his note. Needless to say (as usual in his movies), Woody doesn't get very far.

> ## Dealbreaker Alert
>
> Never hold knowledge of the true extent of your bargaining power in reserve. Tactfully let your opponent know what power you have or you'll lose your negotiating power.

In negotiating terms, Woody's effort failed because his opponents didn't recognize the source of his power—his gun. I'm not advocating that you bring a gun along to your next negotiating session, but you, too, must always make your opponent aware of your bargaining power.

Many negotiators think they should hold knowledge of their power "in reserve" in case it's needed later. Their negotiations usually fail as a result. I recommend never withholding any facts that constitute your negotiating power.

You may, as a matter of strategy, withhold *use* of your power. But even if you do that, you must be absolutely sure your opponent is aware of the full extent of your power.

When you alert your opponent to your bargaining power, do it tactfully. If you hit your opponent over the head with a demonstration of your power he may resent it.

For example, say you're interested in buying a house and you know the seller is having a tough time finding a buyer. If you say, "You can't sell the place, can you?" you may find that the seller will refuse to sell the house to you, even if you're the last buyer on earth. But if you engage in a general, low-key discussion about how many houses there are on the market, and how so many sellers are finding it tough to make a sale, the seller will get your subtle message: that she'll have to give you a bargain to make you sign on the dotted line.

It's All in the Timing: When to Reveal or Use Your Negotiating Power

The key question to ask yourself is: When will revealing or using my power have the greatest impact, and the greatest influence on motivating my opponent to make a deal?

Dealbreaker Alert

If your opponent underestimates your bargaining power, immediately correct her. If you don't, you'll lose your power and weaken your own bargaining position.

In Woody's case, the key was to present the gun before demanding the money. In other negotiations, however, you may not want to reveal or use your power—your connections or your inside knowledge of the situation—before you've built up an understanding with your opponent. As you prepare to bargain and determine the source of your negotiating power, you should also think about the best time to use it.

Develop a game plan during your preparation and decide how and when you'd like to disclose your negotiating power. But keep your plan flexible. Don't lock yourself in.

When the bargaining begins, stay alert to see if your game plan is still the best approach. If it's not, don't hesitate to change directions and reveal or use your power sooner or later. Trust your instincts to decide when time is ripe. The more experience you gain, the more your instincts will be right.

Keep Recharging Your Negotiating Power

Once you've determined and revealed your negotiating power, you have to make sure your opponent is continually aware of it. If your negotiation is high-pressure, protracted, or involves a large exchange of information, your opponent can easily forget about your power. If that happens, your power is useless.

Say you want to hire a contractor to remodel your kitchen—space-age appliances, sky-lights, new cabinets, the works. It's a tremendous job and you know you'll have to haggle over the price. As you prepare to negotiate, you realize that you've got several positions of negotiating power:

➤ You've waited until the winter time, because contractors will be looking for inside work at that time of year.

➤ Your neighbors, the Joneses, are also thinking about remodeling. They've said that they would consider hiring your contractor, if he does a good job on your kitchen.

➤ You're willing to pay 25 percent of the total cost before any work begins, as an added incentive to get a good price.

At your first meeting with the contractor, Rick Wrecker, you reveal your three sources of power. Still, Rick comes back with a price that's too high. You speak with other

121

contractors, get a few more estimates, then decide to see Rick again. How do you remind Rick of your negotiating edge? There are two good ways to keep your power fresh in your opponent's memory.

Repeat Yourself...Repeat Yourself...Repeat Yourself...

Repetition is the best way to remind your opponent of your negotiating power and magnify its impact. Again, this technique involves a little diplomacy and good timing. You want to remind your opponent of your power—not beat him over the head with it.

Dealmaking Tip

Forgetful opponents are common, especially if your opponent is a busy person juggling a lot of balls. So never hesitate to repeat yourself when you bargain. Remind your opponent of your bargaining power—tactfully—every chance you get.

At your second meeting with Rick, for example, you should tactfully repeat your three elements of power to refresh Rick's memory. You could say something like, "I've spoken with quite a few other contractors and they seem eager for this job...between my kitchen and the Joneses', they'll have work lined up for the entire winter."

Questioning Your Power

Another way to keep your bargaining power fresh in your opponent's mind is to ask questions about it. You might ask Rick: "It'll be nice to work inside when the snow is piling up, won't it?" He'll be forced to answer yes, and you will have made your point.

Make sure your questions aren't too obvious—they'll have greater impact and your opponent won't resent you for asking them.

Mental Practice: The Way to Boost Your Negotiating Power

Performing artists and athletes have long known the power of visualizing their performances. You can harness that power to boost your negotiating power, as well.

When you think of "practice," you probably envision physically performing a certain act. When you drive golf balls at a driving range, you're physically practicing your golf game. But mental practice can also improve your performance.

That's important when it comes to negotiation, because you're not going to have an opportunity for a real "dress rehearsal" before you start bargaining. But mental practice can serve the same purpose.

Dealmaking Tip

Remember, when you negotiate, you're pitting your mind against your opponent's. The more you prepare in your mind, the greater negotiating power you'll have.

What Mental Practice Really Means

When you mentally practice, envision yourself at the bargaining table. Think about everything you intend to say and do. Imagine how your opponent might respond. Be specific.

When you get into the actual bargaining, you'll often find that the negotiation will unfold closely to how you've envisioned it. That gives you an edge. In a sense, you've "been there before." With mental rehearsal, the actual negotiation will be easier on your system (you won't be as nervous or stressed out) and you'll enjoy the bargaining process a lot more. Moreover, you'll quickly discover your success ratio will increase dramatically.

It's Been Said

"Knowledge is a treasure but practice is the key to it." —Thomas Fuller

Picture This: A Sample Mental Rehearsal

Say you've decided to go after that long overdue raise. Get comfortable and visualize every detail of the entire bargaining process. Picture yourself walking into the office and making some small talk. Watch yourself confidently launching into your request. (Imagine at least two, preferably three, approaches you'll take. That gives you the flexibility to choose the best approach when you're actually negotiating.) Visualize yourself making good eye contact and sitting up straight like your mother always told you to.

Be realistic, even in your imagination. (How likely is it that your boss will say, "A fifteen-percent raise? Why not make it fifty!"?) Visualize every possible excuse your boss might use to turn you down ("We're under a wage freeze right now," "There's no money for raises—it was a bad year for widgets," etc.) and come up with an answer.

Be graphic. Picture your boss's face and her physical reaction when you pop the question. Visualize the whole event, from start to finish, in great detail.

Finally, imagine your boss saying yes.

Rehearse a half-dozen times or even more until you've got the entire process down cold. When you finally do get to negotiate, you'll be more comfortable, more confident, more powerful, and more likely to get what you want.

The Least You Need to Know

➤ Determine your negotiating power as you prepare to negotiate.

➤ Always make your opponent fully aware of the true extent of your bargaining power even if you don't have to use it.

➤ Reveal or use your power when your instincts tell you the time is ripe.

➤ Repetition and questions are good ways to keep the true extent of your bargaining power fresh in your opponent's mind.

➤ Before you negotiate, mentally rehearse the entire negotiation to increase your negotiating power.

Good Habits, Bad Habits

Think about how many of the things you do are governed by habit. Brushing your teeth, combing your hair, driving to work or school—your brain is on "cruise control" through most or all of these activities. That's because they have become habits.

Habits, as William James points out in his book *The Principles of Psychology*, are nothing more than pathways through your brain. The more you repeat an activity, the deeper the pathway gets. By developing habits, your mind is free to focus on other subjects. But as any of us who have tried to lose weight or stop smoking know, the deeper the pathway, the harder it is to change. In this chapter, you learn how to make the most of your good habits—and minimize or eliminate your bad ones.

The Effects of Habits on Negotiating

Anything can (and often does) happen in negotiation. Good negotiating habits will put you in a better position to deal with the unexpected, because you'll be able to focus on the changing situation without any distractions.

On the other hand, bad negotiating habits will hurt your bargaining position because they'll hinder your performance. For example, if you frequently interrupt when someone else is talking, you'll interrupt during negotiation, too—even though you shouldn't. That works to your disadvantage by causing you to miss important information, and annoys your opponent. Similarly, if you constantly fidget, you'll distract your opponent when you don't want to. That, too, can work to your disadvantage.

Good Negotiating Habits

There are a number of qualities every good negotiator should have. Practice the following good habits every day and they'll spill over into your negotiating:

➤ Make good eye contact with everyone you meet. Looking away from people suggests that you lack confidence—and that's not the impression you want to make when you negotiate!

➤ Dress neatly and professionally.

➤ Speak clearly.

➤ Eliminate "fillers" ("you knows" and "ums") from your conversation.

➤ Listen carefully (no interrupting!) and ask pertinent questions.

➤ Sit with good posture.

➤ Stand and walk with your head up, shoulders back, and body straight.

➤ Develop a standard method of preparation for every meeting and negotiation. (See Chapters 2 and 3.)

➤ If you're chronically late, try to arrive early at all of your appointments. Set your clocks ahead a few minutes (or more!) if you must.

These habits have two immediate benefits. They help you become a good conversationalist, capable of listening carefully, asking pointed questions, and thinking well on your feet. They also help you convey an air of confidence that bolsters your negotiating position. Your confidence makes you seem more believable and your opponent will be more likely to respect and be influenced by your negotiating position.

Hard Habits to Break

Were you ever shocked by the sound of your own voice on someone's answering machine? Have you ever been surprised to catch sight of yourself in a store window? Most of us don't realize the way we appear to others. Many of our bad habits—speaking rapid-fire or in a slow drawl, slouching or hunching over, avoiding eye contact—go unnoticed, unless someone tips us off. And who's willing to do that?

Dealbreaker Alert

You can't carry bad habits around wherever you go and expect them to suddenly disappear when it's time to negotiate.

Unconscious mannerisms can be deadly to effective negotiating. They can make you appear uncomfortable or, even worse, incompetent.

The best way to get rid of your bad habits is quickly and decisively. William James put it this way: "...in the acquisition of a new habit, or the leaving off of an old one, we must...launch ourselves with as strong and decided an initiative as possible...Never suffer an exception to occur till the new habit is securely rooted in your life."

Dealmaking Tip

When you're negotiating, notice any bad habits your opponent has, such as avoiding eye contact. After you've finished negotiating, think about whether you have the same bad habits. That's an excellent way to spot your own bad habits.

A few nasty habits you should immediately eliminate from your negotiating repertoire:

➤ *Fidgeting with pencils, eyeglasses, cups, or anything that distracts your opponent.* I once negotiated with an opponent who beat a pencil on the table like a drummer in a rock band. Your opponent won't concentrate on what you're saying if you're fidgeting while you're talking. (Don't confuse bad habits that disturb your opponent with situations in which you want to effectively break your opponent's concentration. In the latter case, you are taking a deliberate action to achieve a specific result. In the former, you are repeating an unconscious gesture that may jeopardize your bargaining position.)

➤ *Interrupting your opponent.* Ever talk to someone who constantly interrupts? It's annoying. You don't want to frustrate your opponent and perhaps make him angry.

➤ *Using "fillers."* I'm sure you know people whose conversation is perpetually sprinkled with "you know" or "ummmmmm." They don't sound particularly articulate or intelligent, do they? Make some tape recordings of yourself running through your arguments. Play them back and listen carefully. What unnecessary fillers do you rely on? Concentrate on eliminating them from your everyday speech.

➤ *Taking extensive notes.* This isn't a good bargaining practice because it diverts your attention from your opponent. For example, if your opponent makes an offer and then looks away, that's a clue that she lacks confidence in the offer. If you're busy taking notes and miss that small but crucial clue, you might think that your opponent is making a good offer when, in fact, she isn't.

It's Been Said
"Excellence…is not an act but a habit."
—Aristotle

I limit my note-taking to writing down key matters (such as the terms of offers made), or to recording facts or documents that I've promised to find and give to my opponent. Other than that, my pen stays in my pocket.

➤ *Jotting down or reading from notes that your opponent can't see.* Your opponent will get suspicious—even if you're just doodling or writing a grocery list. If you must rely on notes, hold them so your opponent can see what you're doing.

Dealing With Your Opponent's Bad Habits

Your opponent's bad habits make him less effective, but they also prevent you from concentrating on what your opponent is saying. For example, I once had an opponent who liked to click his briefcase latch open and shut. That sound was as inescapable as the ticking of a large clock when you're trying to drop off to sleep.

How do you deal with an opponent who has a distracting bad habit? You can either grin and bear it, or tactfully get your opponent to try and stop it until the bargaining is over. In the briefcase example, for instance, I could have said something like, "That briefcase must be in your way. Would you like me to put it with your coat so you have more room?" If you can break your opponent's bad habit, you can strengthen your concentration and throw your opponent slightly off-balance. This swings the bargaining edge in your favor.

The Least You Need to Know

➤ Good negotiating habits will free your mind to concentrate on the bargaining.

➤ The best way to develop good negotiating habits—such as making good eye contact, standing up straight, and arriving on time—is to practice these good habits even when you're not negotiating.

➤ Eliminate bad negotiating habits—such as fidgeting, taking excessive notes, and using fillers when you speak—quickly and decisively.

➤ If you must ask your opponent to stop a bad habit (such as fiddling with something or smoking), do it tactfully.

Chapter 17

Staying in Control: Controlling the Negotiation Process

In This Chapter

➤ When and how to gain control of the negotiating process

➤ How to use "funneling" to maintain control

➤ Regaining control when you lose it

Nearly every aspect of your life is governed by rules and laws. Legal rights and responsibilities control your actions toward others. Traffic lights and speed limits control the way you drive (I hope). Rules of etiquette prevent you from committing social mistakes.

Negotiation is one of the few exceptions—there are no formal rules of the game. In negotiation, you are guided by your own character, integrity, and honesty. That's why you should try to control the bargaining process. The more you control the bargaining, the more you can steer the discussions toward your negotiating objective—to get what you want. You can focus your thoughts on strategies and techniques, on what you say and how you say it, on reading your opponent's body language and controlling your own. In this chapter, I show you how to control the bargaining process so you have a better chance of getting what you want.

When and How to Get in Control

There are many ways, both before and during negotiation, that you can place yourself in a position of control. I've already mentioned some of them in previous chapters. But control is such an important negotiating asset that it's worth repeating here.

Taking Control Before the Negotiation Begins

You can begin to assert yourself even before you sit down at the bargaining table by controlling the negotiation setting:

➤ Bargain on your home field (see Chapter 4).

➤ Set the negotiation for the time when you are mentally at your sharpest (see Chapter 4).

➤ Mentally rehearse the negotiation (see Chapter 15).

Gaining Control When Negotiation Is Underway

Once you're actually facing your opponent, you can continue to control the bargaining process by:

➤ *Asking questions.* Questions place your opponent on the defensive. When your opponent is answering your questions, she can't ask you questions or focus on her negotiating strategy. I've discussed questions and when and how to use them in Chapter 8.

➤ *Focusing on one issue until it is settled—even if your opponent is trying to skip to another issue.* Salespeople do this all the time. Say you're interested in buying a plush new couch for your living room. The salesman starts hawking a set of matching chairs, coffee table, and lamp. He says he'll sell it to you for a special price as part of a package. You say you don't want to spend that much money. The salesman describes the store's special financing options—instant credit for all you can buy, and you don't have to pay until the year 2001!

Suddenly, instead of focusing on pricing the couch, you're hip-deep in discussing an entire room renovation. A lot of people would get sucked into buying these new items. Don't let it happen to you. Keep your eyes on the prize and say firmly, "No thanks. All the room needs right now is a couch. How much is it?" And start pulling out your wallet. That will keep both of you focused on your primary negotiating base (discussed in Chapter 2) and help you maintain control of the negotiation.

Dealbreaker Alert

Failure to maintain your primary base (your bargaining objective) is directly proportionate to how complex the bargaining issues are. The more complicated the issues are, the greater the danger you'll lose sight of your base. That's why you should firmly tattoo your base in your mind, especially when you prepare.

➤ *Not raising new issues once the bargaining begins.* This needlessly broadens the discussions and creates an air of uncertainty.

➤ *Not introducing any new parties or new elements once the bargaining begins.* If you do, it gives your opponent a perfect opportunity to raise new ideas or even have second thoughts on issues already agreed upon.

Let's Talk Terms
New elements are people, ideas, or issues that are foreign to either the negotiators or the subject under negotiation. If you raise a new issue or introduce a new person into the bargaining after it's started, that's a new element.

Funneling: A Negotiation Technique, Not a New Sport

Funneling is a way of ensuring that closed issues stay closed. It adds to your negotiating control because it prevents you from having to reopen or rehash issues that have already been settled.

The more negotiating experience you gain, the better you'll become at funneling. When your opponent tries to reopen a closed issue (they often do), tactfully remind him that the point has been settled. If he still insists on discussing the issue, quickly explain what the agreement on the issue was. Then move on to something else. Don't allow yourself or your opponent to begin discussing and renegotiating the closed issue.

Let's Talk Terms
Funneling means setting aside points once they are resolved. They may be returned to later in the negotiation for review or summation—but *not* to renegotiate.

Dealbreaker Alert

The more parties involved in the bargaining, the more likely old issues will be rehashed, and the more difficult it will be for you to maintain control.

You're Out of Control! How to Regain Negotiating Control if You Lose It

Ever lose an argument with your kids, your spouse, or your boss? Then you know the sinking feeling that accompanies a loss of control. You're on the defensive, struggling to explain yourself, stammering for answers as you get bombarded with questions. You may find yourself sidetracked onto an issue that has nothing to do with the one you want to discuss. Everything you say is misinterpreted. You can't win.

When you lose negotiating control, you're most vulnerable to making concessions. Before that happens, you must regain control—and the quicker the better.

Dealmaking Tip

It's almost always better to act than to react. When you act you're on the offense. When you react you're on the defense—and that's not where you want to be when you bargain.

Once you've lost control of the bargaining, there are ways to regain it:

➤ Immediately ask for a recess or "time-out." Then reassess the bargaining and think about what went wrong and how you can remedy it.

➤ Look for ways to take the offense.

➤ Immediately after the recess, start by summarizing what's happened in the bargaining process to date. That will help give you control. Once you've finished with your summary, begin to launch your own bargaining position(s). You're now back in control of the negotiation.

The Least You Need to Know

➤ The more you can control the bargaining, the greater your chances of getting what you want.

➤ Prior to the negotiation, you can gain control by choosing the place and time for negotiation and mentally rehearsing the negotiation.

➤ During negotiation, you can gain and maintain control by asking questions, avoiding new elements, and funneling the discussion.

➤ When you sense you've lost control, ask for a recess. Use your recess time to figure out what went wrong and why.

➤ Two good ways to regain control are to restart the bargaining by summarizing the negotiation to date, and then to start off with your own bargaining position(s).

Part 5
Overcoming Problems in Negotiation

You're going to encounter problems when you bargain. There's no way to avoid them. Negotiating difficulties are kind of like mosquitoes on a hot, muggy day—the more you swat at them, the more you are attacked. Or so it seems.

In this part, you discover the many tools you can use to help overcome some common negotiating problems. You learn how to ease through the bargaining process with fewer headaches—and maybe even start to have some fun!

Handling Anger in Negotiation

I once represented a client who was involved in a three-car accident, but wasn't at fault. Another driver—let's call him Crash Carson—was the true instigator of the accident.

My opponent, who represented Crash's insurance company, refused to admit that my client was not in the wrong. He insisted that I cut the amount of settlement money I was asking for.

I held my ground, tactfully insisting that the amount was reasonable because his client was at fault. I could see his anger and frustration building as he realized I was not going to give way. Finally, he erupted, pounding his fist on my desk and yelling, "Okay! My driver caused the $#@!$# wreck. So what?! I'm still not paying what you want!" Then he threw his papers in his briefcase and stomped out.

It's rare to get an opponent to admit liability, and it would never have happened if my opponent hadn't gotten so angry. His temper was my ally. Within a week I received a check for the full amount for my client.

There's a saying that the person who angers you, conquers you. That's what happened to my opponent. In this chapter, you learn what to do if anger—yours or your opponent's—disrupts the negotiation.

How Anger Disrupts Negotiation

Anger has many physiological effects on your body. When you get angry, your blood pressure rises and your heart rate increases.

The behavioral consequences of anger aren't pretty, either. You can't think or act logically when you are angry, and usually, nothing you do when you're angry is particularly constructive. In negotiating, anger has two downsides, which are described in the following sections.

Vengeance Is Mine!

Usually, anger is supplanted by a desire for revenge. (Think scorned girlfriend Glenn Close killing the rabbit in *Fatal Attraction*.)

Once you're set on revenge, chances are good you'll say or do something that will jeopardize your bargaining position. It happens all the time, as my insurance man story shows. Just think of some of the things you've blurted out in anger in personal relationships and you'll know what I mean.

Dealbreaker Alert

The person who gets angry during negotiation usually loses—either because a favorable agreement is not reached, the negotiation is terminated entirely, or he or she makes a damaging admission while angry.

My Way or the Highway

Anger may also make you obstinate. Once you're angry, you may become stubbornly insistent on all your negotiating positions, allowing no room for concession or bargaining. You may become unwilling to countenance any changes, even reasonable ones. You can see how this makes you difficult to negotiate with.

The general rule is: Never become angry when you're bargaining. Stay cool even if your opponent says or does something designed to provoke your anger. Here are a few ways to stay cool in the midst of a hot situation:

➤ Take a deep breath and count to ten.

➤ Suggest a five-minute break. Take a walk, drink some cold water, give yourself a chance to calm down.

➤ If your opponent gets personal, say that you are negotiating issues and that personal remarks are not appropriate. (See Chapter 20 for more on personality and principle conflicts and how to handle them.)

When It's OK to Get Angry—the "Controlled Anger" Technique

Based on the previous paragraphs, you might think that there is never a place for anger in negotiation. But there is one very potent exception. You can use anger in a negotiating technique I call "controlled anger."

If your opponent says or does something that fully justifies your anger, keep your cool—but fake anger. Speak and act like you're angry—frown, speak in a tight, stern voice, and use commanding gestures (discussed in Chapter 6).

Use the controlled anger technique when you don't want to be taken for a pushover. It allows you to display your displeasure over your opponent's tactics—without letting you fall victim to the drawbacks of real anger.

It's Been Said
"Heads are wisest when they are cool."
—Ralph Bunche

I once assisted in a negotiation that had drawn out over a long period of time with no progress. I was asked to assist a man who was selling a company.

Many corporate buyouts are subject to delays, because the "buyers" aren't really that serious about buying and actually have other motives in mind—such as learning as much as possible about the other company. (That's called "going to school.") Usually, the more drawn out the bargaining, the more the "buyers" can learn. Once the pseudo-"buyers" have discovered all they need to know, they either drop the talks or make such far-out proposals that the other side walks away.

It's Been Said
"Anger is momentary madness, so control your passion or it will control you."
—Horace, *Epistles*

I suspected that my opponent was deliberately stalling because he was not responding to my client's proposals or making any proposals of his own. The discussions were going nowhere. That gave me a good reason to get angry and my opponent knew it.

So I did get angry—but with controlled anger. I kept my emotions under complete control. Only my voice, gestures, and facial expressions revealed my displeasure. I advised my opponent that my client intended to walk away from the bargaining unless meaningful proposals were laid down on the table. That did it. The bargaining got down to serious business.

You should realize that controlled anger has its limits. I had to limit my controlled anger to my opponent's delaying tactics. If I had gone too far, my opponent would have had full justification to get angry at me, and that would have jeopardized my client's interests. By controlling my anger, I turned my opponent's delaying tactic into a bargaining advantage for my client.

Controlled anger can be risky, so use it judiciously. Be certain that your anger is justified, and limit your controlled anger only to the issues that justify it.

If Your Opponent Gets Angry

If you're stuck in a negotiation that has reached a standstill, and you have no other way of breaking the log jam, your opponent's anger might be just the dynamite to do it.

Angry people frequently say and do things that they shouldn't—that's why you may want to get your opponent angry. But be careful. If you decide to provoke your opponent's anger, you don't want to get that person so worked up that the negotiation is terminated.

Usually, when the discussions are at a standstill, both you and your opponent are prone to getting angry because you'll each blame the other for blocking progress. This is where you have to keep your cool.

Testing Your Opponent's Reactions

In some situations, you can tactfully state that your opponent's "unreasonableness" is what is blocking the agreement. Notice how mild and tame the word "unreasonableness" is—it's not provocative enough to infuriate your opponent, but it may be severe enough to get him to break the stalemate.

Or, you might contend that your opponent never really intended to reach a "fair and reasonable" agreement. What you're really saying is that your opponent is not a fair and reasonable person. Most people consider themselves to be fair and reasonable, so this approach will usually cause your opponent to launch into a lengthy explanation of why she *is* being fair—and she may even suggest a fine deal in order to prove it.

> **Dealbreaker Alert**
>
> Once you've lit your opponent's fuse, be a good listener! If you interrupt at this stage, you risk provoking your opponent to uncontrollable anger—and that's not what you want to deal with.

You also might want to get your opponent angry when he is holding a far stronger bargaining position—most if not all the aces—and you're searching for a way to weaken your opponent's hand and strengthen yours.

I once represented a client who was an investor in a real estate development. He wasn't happy with the way the development was progressing and he wanted out of the deal, but he had no legal means of getting out.

Even though my client had a legally weak position, I kept pushing the developer to cut my client loose, on my terms. My sheer persistence won the day. The developer got angry at me and he finally gave in to the deal I was proposing.

Here again, frame your remarks mildly. Your goal is to make your opponent mildly angry, not uncontrollably enraged.

> **It's Been Said**
> "If anger proceeds from a great cause, it turns to fury; if from a small cause, it is peevishness; and so is always either terrible or ridiculous."
> —Jeremy Taylor

One Way to Guarantee a Fight at the Bargaining Table

Whenever you deliberately make your opponent angry you take a risk. Everybody's fuse ignites differently—some opponents will fly into a tantrum at the slightest provocation, others will take a lot more before they lose their temper. So try to gauge your opponent's boiling point before you attempt to provoke him.

As you learned in Chapter 12, one potent way to provoke your opponent is to make a personal slight that attacks his "self." The closer anything you say touches upon your opponent's self, the more likely your opponent will become genuinely, irrevocably angry.

Dealbreaker Alert

Confine your remarks to the subject matter of the negotiation. If you broaden them and get into areas beyond what you're negotiating, you run the risk of inadvertently setting off your opponent's fuse.

For example, if your opponent is a real estate agent, any snide comments you make about the real estate market in general may be enough to provoke him to mild anger. Take a crack at the real estate agency he works for and you come one step closer to touching his self. Disparage his abilities to do his job, and you've made direct contact with his self. Now you're risking genuine anger that will only make negotiation more difficult (if not impossible). You don't want to go this far.

When you decide to deliberately provoke your opponent's anger, always consider how close to his self your actions or remarks will get. Personal attacks have no place in successful negotiation.

Calming Your Opponent Down

If your opponent gets uncontrollably angry with you, there are five approaches you can take to calm the situation down.

➤ Anger is a temporary emotion, and it's usually entirely curable by a good dose of time. If your opponent is mildly upset, a short break will be fine. If you think a little more time is necessary, let your opponent cool off over lunch or overnight. If your opponent is truly angry, you should allow a few days or a week to pass. Eventually your opponent may even feel foolish about becoming angry.

➤ Show that there's no reason for your opponent's anger (if this is indeed the case). Explain that there was no insult intended by your actions or remarks.

➤ Remedy the situation. If you've somehow personally slighted your opponent, a simple, sincere apology will do. Don't be reluctant to apologize and don't let pride or stubbornness stand in your way. Admitting fault is not a sign of weakness—it's good negotiating. You're there to successfully negotiate something important to you. Stay focused on that objective.

➤ If your opponent is furious over something you've said or done, you may have to make a concession or two to regain his goodwill and get the negotiating back on course. This is risky because your opponent may construe your concessions as a sign of weakness and may demand even more from you. So use this approach only when you've exhausted all of your other options.

➤ Send someone to bargain in your place. However, this is risky because it can be interpreted as an admission that you were in the wrong. If your opponent has any kind of bargaining skills, she'll start asking for large concessions.

Say your car is five days out of the shop and it's already making that strange pinging noise again. Disgustedly, you take your car back to Rocky's Repairs, where Rocky tells you it's a new, more intricate and costly problem than the one he's fixed before. You've already paid for the first set of repairs and you don't want to pay anything more. Rocky says, "Too bad." In a surge of anger, you accuse Rocky of running an incompetent shop. Rocky's shop is part of Rocky's self, so now you've accused Rocky himself of being incompetent. And he doesn't take that lightly.

It's Been Said
"Time heals what reason cannot."
—Seneca

That's enough to bring the negotiating process to a grinding halt (no pun intended). You still have the pinging car and Rocky still has your money. The stalemate will continue until you can calm him down.

The passage of time will help. Ask Rocky if you can come back in two or three days. If he refuses, apologize for losing your cool. Then point out that it's really in both of your best interests to reach a friendly solution—you'll have a well-running car, and Rocky will have a satisfied customer.

Once you've rescheduled, do nothing. Let time be your ally. It'll eliminate a lot of Rocky's anger. When you next show up at Rocky's Repairs, immediately offer an apology. If you think it's necessary, go further and throw in an explanation for your bad behavior. Say you were having a bad day, or that your car is vital to your life and you were frustrated by its problems. Any legitimate, genuine explanation will help get rid of Rocky's anger.

Then, explain again why you're there, to either get your car back in working order or get your money back.

Once Rocky is calm, be extra careful not to get him angry again. It's difficult enough to assuage an opponent once—it's nearly impossible to do it twice.

Dealbreaker Alert

Effective negotiation is knowing how to make your point without making the opponent your enemy. A twice-angered opponent will be your enemy.

The Least You Need to Know

➤ Except for very special situations, anger disrupts negotiation by making both you and your opponent vengeful and obstinate.

➤ If your opponent gives you cause, use the "controlled anger" technique to express your displeasure.

➤ If your negotiation has reached a stalemate, you might try to mildly provoke your opponent in order to break the impasse.

➤ Avoid making personal attacks on your opponent. They may irreparably damage the negotiation.

➤ If your opponent becomes genuinely angry, take a break, apologize, or show that your opponent's anger is unjustified. As a last resort, you may have to make concessions to assuage your opponent.

Chapter 19

Fear in Negotiation

In This Chapter

➤ The effects of fear

➤ The three most common negotiating fears

➤ How you can increase your opponent's fears to help you get what you want

➤ How to avoid being manipulated by fear

Every week, a kindergarten teacher I know visits the local library to check out a load of books for all her students. At one point, the librarian complained about all the books she was checking out. My friend offered a solution: How about if she brought all 20 of her kindergartners in to scramble around and look for their own books? The librarian never complained again.

That's a sweet, simple lesson on the power of fear. What could be more frightening to a librarian than the thought of 20 five-year-olds zooming through her library? Not much. In this chapter, you learn how fear affects negotiation.

It's Been Said
"Men's actions depend to a great extent upon fear."
—John F. Milburn

The Effects of Fear

You learned about the powerful effects of fear at an early age. Think about how you feared your first day of school, the first time you drove a car, the night of your first big date. Fear still accompanies you on many occasions such as job interviews, opening-night performances, and wedding days, to name only a few.

When we fear something, we imagine the worst. That's a powerful motivator to act. Think about your first date. You were afraid you'd sprout a noxious pimple before the big night, so you took extra-careful care of your skin. You didn't want your date to think you looked like a geek, so you chose your clothes with extra care.

Fear also shows up when you negotiate. The more important the negotiation, the greater your fear will be.

Fear and Negotiation

I had my first brush with fear when I was a negotiating aide fresh out of law school. My job was to collect debts for a large car dealership (and you think your job is awful).

Many of the debtors weren't paying up, and I wasn't sure how I could force them to pay without getting involved in a lot of messy, time-consuming lawsuits.

I managed to motivate most of them to pay out of fear. I constructed a simple letter that consisted of only two sentences. The first acknowledged the amount of the debt. The second read as follows:

> "If payment is not received within two weeks, appropriate action will be taken which will result in additional expenses to you, the debtor."

What was "appropriate action"? What were the "additional expenses"? I deliberately left those phrases vague—I wanted the debtor's imagination to run wild over the possibilities. My tactic worked. Within a few days, the checks started arriving in the mail.

Dealmaking Tip

Fear is a state of mind. You can overcome fear in negotiation by replacing it with positive thoughts.

The Top Three Negotiating Fears

The fears you'll face in negotiation usually center around three subjects:

➤ Fear of loss

➤ Fear of the unknown

➤ Fear of failure

Two of those fears motivated my dealership debtors to pay up. They feared both the "additional expenses" (fear of loss of money) and what the "appropriate action" would be (fear of the unknown). Let's take a closer look at each.

Fear of Loss

Many negotiations hinge on the fear of losing something of value—money, a dream house, a raise, or even a good deal.

Crafty negotiators know how to harp on our fears of missing out on a good thing. Stockbrokers call with promises of investments that will double your money. Landlords tell you that several other people want the apartment, so you'd better sign the lease fast. Store advertisements trumpet "unbeatable, one-day-only" sale prices.

Every negotiation that involves something of value will make both you and your opponent highly prone to fear of loss. For example, you finally find your dream home. The broker tells you several other buyers are ready to make offers on the house.

That revelation is a deliberate ploy to motivate you to make an immediate offer—maybe one that's higher than the seller's asking price. I cover how you can protect yourself from experiencing fear of loss from such tactics when buying a home in Chapter 23.

Here are some tips that will help you when you face losing a deal you very much want:

➤ Never give your opponent any hint that you have a great desire to make the deal (buy the house, take the job, sell your car for the opponent's price, etc.).

➤ Be mentally prepared to walk away from the deal if it's not what you want.

➤ Find an alternate solution before you bargain (a comparable house, another prospective job, another potential car buyer, etc.). That will help prevent you from experiencing fear of loss—you'll know that if this particular deal doesn't go your way, there will be others.

Fear of the Unknown

When you fear the unknown, you imagine the worst. (If you're like me, you probably experience this every time you visit your doctor or dentist.) As far as negotiation is concerned, fear of the unknown is a great motivator. What if the home sellers laugh at your offer? What if your negotiating opponent turns you down flat?

Here are some tips on how you can conquer your fear of the unknown:

➤ Prepare thoroughly. It'll give you confidence—and fear can't survive in the face of confidence.

➤ Remind yourself that most, if not all, of the horrible outcomes you are imagining will never happen. Sweep away those fears by concentrating on your preparation and strategies.

➤ Again, find an alternate solution before you bargain.

➤ And again, be prepared to walk away from the deal.

Fear of Failure

All negotiators, even the most experienced and most prepared, have a slight panic attack before stepping in to a new negotiation. That's natural. Negotiating is a performance, like acting or speaking in public, and a little "performance anxiety" is understandable.

There are several ways to deal with this fear:

➤ Acknowledge your fear instead of repressing it. But don't get obsessive.

➤ Prepare thoroughly and examine the negotiation from as many angles as possible. The more you know, the less you will fear being caught off-guard during the negotiation. (See Chapters 2 and 3 for more on preparation.)

➤ Mentally rehearse your negotiation before you go in (as explained in Chapter 15).

➤ Dress for the negotiation in clothes that make you feel good about yourself.

➤ Make sure your notes or files (if you have them) are in order before you begin.

➤ Act confident. Your opponent won't detect your fear unless you show it. Take deep breaths so your voice is controlled and firm, not shaky. Stand up straight. Make good eye contact.

It's Been Said
"The only thing we have to fear is fear itself. "
—Franklin D. Roosevelt

148

The Fear Tactic

We all know how to use fear to get what we want. Parents warn their children, "No fighting...or else!" Police officers threaten to revoke licenses. Lawyers threaten to sue. And skilled negotiators may (tactfully) paint a picture that creates fear and motivates you to agree to their positions. Unskilled negotiators may bluntly say, "Take it or leave it!" because they know that you want the deal.

A photographer I know was desperate to collect overdue bills. He hit upon a fear-inducing solution. He leafed through his files and found the most unflattering picture he had for every deadbeat customer. He attached each picture to each bill—along with a note suggesting that if he received permission to display the terrible picture in his window, he'd consider the bill paid in full. The customers—afraid of having every wrinkle and double chin prominently displayed in the store window—paid up quickly after that.

Stay alert during the bargaining to pick up clues as to how badly your opponent wants to close the deal. If your opponent is afraid of losing the deal, you can add more demands without worrying about the deal falling through.

Here are some tips on how you can spot your opponent's strong desire to clinch the deal:

➤ Your opponent was the one who initiated the bargaining (for example, he approached you about buying your home or car).

➤ Your opponent makes an offer or counteroffer that's especially generous—more than you expected.

➤ Your opponent quickly responds to any suggestion you make that indicates you're not certain about completing the deal (for example, if you say, "I'm not so sure I want to sell" or "I'm not in a hurry to buy right now.").

➤ Your opponent doesn't protest when you make a far-out proposal.

The "Greater Fear" Technique

This technique will work in any negotiation in which your opponent is likely to play on your fears.

Let's use buying a car as an example (now there's a scary experience). At the dealership, you see a car you like, but you want to shop around before you make a decision. The salesperson tells you that the special sale on the model you want ends tomorrow, so if you don't sign now you could lose out on a great deal. That's a subtle way of saying, "You better buy the car today or else," and is designed to cause you fear of loss.

Many people might take the bait. But you're prepared—you realize that this is the perfect time to use the "greater fear" technique. You know the salesperson works on a commission and is anxious to make the sale. So you tell the salesperson you're sure other dealers will meet and even beat his price. Now the salesperson is afraid of losing the sale, and you're in a position to get an even greater discount than advertised.

Let's take another example. You decide to stop payment on the out-of-control computer you bought at Erratic Electronics. The store owner threatens to turn the matter over to a collection agency if you don't pay up. He mentions how a nonpayment notice will badly damage your credit rating.

You advise the store owner that if he jeopardizes your credit rating, you'll report the bad workmanship and unhelpful service to the Better Business Bureau—and, if absolutely necessary, take legal action for damaging your credit rating without cause. You're now in a good position to get a new computer.

Fear and Time

Fear diminishes with time. If your opponent is afraid of losing the deal, take every opportunity to tactfully remind him that the deal may not go through. The longer the negotiation takes, the more times you should remind your opponent of his fears.

Never Let Them See You Sweat—How to Remain Unaffected by Fear

Never, never, never let your opponent know that you want to seal a deal, no matter how desperate you may be. Let's return to the home-buying example. The real estate agent takes you through the house. Your spouse praises the backyard. You ooh and ahh over the working fireplace. You both mention how anxious you are to move.

You've both just tipped off the salesperson that you're strongly attached to the house and fear losing it. The salesperson takes advantage of your fear by telling you that the house will be shown to several other couples that very day. Faced with the possibility of losing that home, the chances are good that you will be motivated to buy the house for more than what you wanted to pay.

Dealbreaker Alert

A skillful opponent will frequently probe during bargaining to see how badly you want to close the deal so he can take advantage of your fear of loss. Stay alert and don't tip your hand.

The best way to protect yourself from this kind of manipulation is to never disclose, by either your words or acts, that you're strongly attached to whatever you're bargaining for. Don't praise any aspects of the deal in front of your opponent; don't express delight. Keep as bland a poker face as you can. This will prevent your opponent from cashing in on your fears.

> **It's Been Said**
> "The proper course with every kind of fear is to think about it rationally and calmly, and with great concentration, until it has become completely familiar. In the end familiarity will blunt its terrors."
> —Bertrand Russell

The Least You Need to Know

➤ Fear motivates us to act.

➤ The three most common fears you'll encounter when you negotiate are the fear of loss, the fear of the unknown, and the fear of failure.

➤ Recognizing your opponent's fears will increase your chances of negotiating successfully.

➤ Use the "greater fear" technique when an opponent tries to manipulate you through fear.

➤ Avoid displaying your fears during negotiation. Keep a poker face and carefully monitor what you say about the deal.

Chapter 20

Getting Personal: When Principles or Personalities Collide

In This Chapter

➤ What to do when your opponent gets personal

➤ What to do when your opponent stands on a matter of principle

➤ Why you should never attack your opponent's principles

I once negotiated to buy a business. The seller wasn't happy with the way the deal was progressing, and he began to make snide comments about lawyers—knowing full well that I was one.

I remained calm, smiled slightly, and made the mild observation that most lawyers are good, hard-working people trying their best to represent their clients; but, like any other profession, there probably were a few rotten apples in the bunch.

That took the wind out of my opponent's sails and got our discussions back on track. In this chapter, I show you how to handle negotiations that get too personal.

Let's Talk Terms

Personality is used here in its broadest sense, as defined in *Webster's New World Dictionary*: "The distinctive individual qualities of a person, considered collectively."

The Risks of Getting Personal

No matter how tempted you are (and how much justification you may have), never make a personal attack on your opponent. If you do, it will threaten all the goodwill, respect, and diplomacy you've brought to the negotiation thus far, and it may prevent your opponent from wanting to work with you.

Keeping your emotions to yourself is easier said than done. You may be deeply offended if boss turns you down for a raise, a client laughs at your proposal, or the driver who smashed your fender claims that your driving is at fault.

It can be especially tempting to get personal if you're bargaining with someone close to you, such as a family member or friend (rather than a business associate). It's easier to get personal when the restraints of polite office behavior are removed.

If you feel you're about to lose control, take a break, take a deep breath, or get a drink of water. Do something—anything—that calms you down and prevents you from personally attacking your opponent. You've got to resist the temptation, no matter how difficult it is, and even if your opponent gives you full justification—like my opponent did with his unpleasant lawyer-bashing.

Take the high road and follow the golden rule: "Do unto others as you would have them do unto you." It's not a sign of weakness, it's a sign of inner strength—and great negotiating skill.

If you can overcome your temptation to attack your opponent personally, you'll be in total command of both yourself and the negotiation. The bargaining momentum will be all yours.

Five Things You Should Never Mention When You Negotiate

Never let the negotiation disintegrate into an insult contest. Avoid any mention of personal characteristics of your opponent, from sly insinuations to outright barbs. Those characteristics include any reference to your opponent's:

➤ Appearance, personal hygiene, or clothing

➤ Race, gender, ethnic background, or religion

➤ Profession, company, or business

➤ Competence or experience

➤ Age

Five Things You Should Never Do When You Negotiate

As you learned in Chapter 6, body language can communicate just as clearly as words. Avoid all physical gestures that translate into, "Your proposals are a joke, you stupid idiot." Aside from the time-honored upraised middle finger, you should avoid:

➤ Exasperated eye-rolling

➤ Disdainful sneering à la Elvis

➤ Finger-pointing or fist-shaking

➤ Book, paper, or furniture throwing

➤ Any gesture your opponent can construe as physically threatening

If you do attack your opponent personally, you'd better be prepared for a searing counter-attack. Don't escalate the verbal war! Stop it right there. Offer an apology—say something like, "Look, I was out of line. We're here to work out a deal, not insult each other. Why don't we take a break and try to talk this over again." Usually that'll do the trick, especially if you combine a gracious apology with a little self-deprecating humor.

Managing an Opponent Who's Become Personal

I've had more than one opponent call me names my publisher won't allow me to print here. I practiced what I'm now preaching—I stayed cool, gently smiled, and said, "I'm sorry you feel that way. I hope we can put this behind us and arrive at a fair resolution." In most cases, we did.

So what can you do when faced with an opponent who calls you a jerk or worse?

➤ Don't join in, no matter how witty your comeback. Remember, your goal is to get what you want, not conduct a verbal war.

➤ Think about the consequences if the negotiation breaks down—you won't get to buy the house, you'll lose the client, your boss will fire you. That alone should be enough to convince you to rescue the situation.

➤ If you can't figure out why your opponent is getting personal, ask. Say something like, "I thought we were discussing a deal here. Why are you getting so offensive?" Maybe something you've said or done has touched a nerve in your opponent. Get the cause out on the table.

➤ If an apology is in order, make it.

➤ If there's a misunderstanding, discuss it and clear it up.

Remember, if your opponent deliberately provokes you, nothing will be more difficult or disconcerting for him than your cool, fair, and impartial reaction. Your control will disarm him. It will make him feel foolish, and in most cases, bring him back to his senses.

Neutralizing Personality Conflicts

On occasion, you'll bargain with an opponent whose personality clashes with yours. That can make it difficult for the two of you to even sit in the same room together, let alone try to work out a deal. Here are some tips on how to handle a personality conflict:

➤ *Stay low-key.* Moderate your tone of voice and your attitude. That will make you less threatening to your opponent, and will help minimize the personality differences between the two of you.

➤ *Be frank.* Tell your opponent that although neither of you seems to have much in common, that's no reason why you can't reach a satisfactory agreement.

➤ *Use the magic words "fair and reasonable."* Tell your opponent that, whatever your personal differences, you know your opponent is "fair and reasonable" and so are you.

A Matter of Principle

I once negotiated with an opponent who made it clear that he never discussed business after 6 p.m. For him, closing business at that hour was a matter of principle. Maybe he felt that way because of family commitments, or religious beliefs, or some other reason. I didn't ask—I didn't have to. I knew from experience that when he uttered the words "a matter of principle" he meant it. If I insisted on bargaining beyond 6 p.m. he would be in no mood to gratify my request. So whenever I negotiated with him, I made sure that when the clock neared 6 p.m., we quit for the day and planned to resume some other time—even if we weren't finished negotiating.

Let's Talk Terms
Webster's New World Dictionary defines *principle* as "A fundamental truth, law, etc. upon which others are based; a rule of conduct; or adherence to such rules; integrity."

When you negotiate, you may not always agree with your opponent's principles, but that's not important. What is important is to understand that your chances of changing your opponent's principles are slim to none. So don't try.

Never, I repeat, never attack your opponent's principles—even if you think your opponent is naive or deluded. If you attack your opponent's principles, you're attacking the inner core of your opponent's self, and you can kiss any bargaining progress good-bye.

How to Overcome Matters of Principle

If your opponent is insistent on a trivial point, concede the point. Don't jeopardize the entire negotiation by trying to force your opponent to surrender a principle for a point that's not important. I routinely concede unimportant matters almost every time I negotiate. It's a great strategy. It promotes progress and makes my opponent feel good, and it paves the way for further negotiating progress.

It's Been Said
"If principle is good for anything, it is worth living up to."
—Benjamin Franklin

If your opponent is immovable on a major bargaining point because of her principles, you have three options:

➤ Concede the point (the most dissatisfying option).

➤ Prove that the point doesn't apply to your opponent's principle.

➤ Find a way around your opponent's principle.

I once negotiated an allocation of about $50,000 to make improvements on a residential development. My opponent stubbornly refused to pay any of the $50,000 and said that, for him, not paying was "a matter of principle." He had never done it before, and he wasn't about to now. As he spoke, his jaw clenched and his face turned red. He was drawing a line in the sand and wanted me to know it.

Bargaining, at that point, came to a halt. I couldn't attack his principle. That would have made him even more furious. I didn't want to concede the point, either ($50,000 is a lot of money!). But I still had those two other options to try.

It's Been Said
"Nothing in this world can take the place of persistence. Talent will not; nothing is more common than unsuccessful men with talent. Genius will not; unrewarded genius is almost a proverb. Education will not; the world is full of educated derelicts. Persistence and determination alone are omnipotent. The slogan "Press on" has solved and always will solve the problems of the human race."
—Calvin Coolidge

First I tried to show him that his principle didn't apply. I pointed out that the improvements I wanted him to pay for would also benefit the neighboring property—which he also owned. By paying $50,000 now, he could actually save some money down the road. That didn't phase him. He repeated he'd never paid for these kind of improvements before and he wouldn't start now.

That left me with the second option—to find a way around our disagreement that satisfied both of us. I proposed that he not pay the $50,000 (so his principle remained intact), but that we receive a $50,000 cut in the purchase price of the development. He agreed, my persistence paid off, and the stalemate was broken.

When All Else Fails...

What if you simply cannot overcome the conflicts that you face with your opponent? If you've tried every suggestion recommended in this chapter and you still can't reach an agreement, there are professionals who can help you finalize the negotiation:

➤ A *mediator* is a neutral third party who is trained in conflict resolution and who makes suggestions and proposals to help you reach an agreement with your opponent. Mediators are commonly used to help negotiate divorce settlements.

➤ An *arbitrator* is another neutral third party who can resolve disputes. When a case is brought before an arbitrator, both parties agree in advance to be bound by the arbitrator's decision. Arbitration is commonly used to settle labor agreements and construction contracts.

For more information about mediators and arbitrators, call or write the following organizations:

➤ American Arbitration Association
140 West 51st Street, New York, NY 10020
(212) 484-4041

➤ National Academy of Arbitrators
Office of the Secretary, 20 Thornwood Drive, Suite 107, Ithaca NY 14850
(607) 257-9925

➤ Academy of Family Mediators
1500 South Highway 100, Suite 355, Golden Valley, MN 55416
(612) 525-8760

The Least You Need to Know

➤ Never attack your opponent personally, even when you have just cause. Avoid insults or threatening gestures.

➤ If your opponent gets personal, don't retaliate. Stay cool, resolve the misunderstanding, or apologize, if necessary.

➤ Neutralize personality conflicts by staying low-key, concentrating on the business at hand, and reminding your opponent that you both are "fair and reasonable" people.

➤ If your opponent is insistent on a trivial point as a matter of principle, concede the point.

➤ If your opponent insists on a major point as a matter of principle, never attack the principle. Try to show why the principle doesn't apply or find a way around it.

Part 6
Sealing the Deal

Offers and counteroffers are sort of like marriage proposals. First, it takes a little courting (bargaining). Then, you have to say the right words at the right time if you want your opponent to say "yes" to your proposal.

As in a marriage proposal, the offer and counteroffer stage is a critical part of the bargaining process. One wrong move or badly timed gesture and the whole negotiation is off—and all your bargaining has gone down the drain.

Closing, too, is a key part of the bargaining process. If you can't close, you're just talking, not bargaining. In this part, I explain how to make offers and counteroffers and seal the deal.

Chapter 21

Making Offers and Counteroffers

In This Chapter

➤ Guidelines for making offers and counteroffers

➤ How to handle your opponent's offers and counteroffers

➤ Highballing and lowballing

➤ Dealmakers and dealbreakers

➤ Effects of making the first large concession

When you make an offer or counteroffer, you put your beliefs on the line. You say, in essence, "This is my proposal and what I *believe* is a fair bargain." You commit yourself to a course of action. If your opponent accepts, the deal is done.

In this chapter, I show you strategies and techniques so you can sail through the offer and counteroffer stage with confidence.

The Negotiation Tango

The offer and counteroffer stage resembles a rumba—there's plenty of motion, but a limited number of steps you can take. After the first offer has been made, you and your opponent can choose one of three maneuvers:

➤ Reject the offer on the table.

➤ Accept the offer on the table and seal the deal.

➤ Propose a counteroffer.

Later in this chapter, you'll see why the last option is almost always the one to go with. But you need to have an offer on the table first.

Let Your Opponent Make the First Move

There's no rule that says which side has to make the first offer, but you'll benefit if you let your opponent do it. Here's why:

➤ When your opponent makes the first offer, she sets the upper or lower limit. Say you want to sell your used car for $6,000. You find an interested buyer and name your price. Now you've set the upper limit. What if the buyer had been willing to pay $6,500? You'd never get it. And if the buyer has any sense at all, she'll already be trying to negotiate down from $6,000.

Likewise, if you're the buyer and you offer $6,000, that's the lowest you can expect to pay. The seller is going to bargain to work up from that figure.

➤ When your opponent leads with the first offer, you immediately have the three options I mentioned earlier open to you. You're always in a good bargaining position when you have plenty of options.

It's like an old story about the medieval serf who was sentenced to death by the king. The serf promised to teach the king's horse how to fly if the king let him live for another year. The king agreed. The serf's friends said he was crazy because horses can't fly. The serf pointed out to his friend that in a year the king might die, the horse might die, or, hey!—maybe he'd even figure out how to make the horse fly.

Three Opening Move Strategies: The Good, The Bad, and The Ugly

Say you've found someone who wants to buy your house. If you want to get the top price, it's important that you begin the bargaining with the right approach. Here are three ways you can proceed, which is best, and why.

The Ugly Opening Move

Buyer: "How much do you want for the property?"

You: "$150,000."

With one utterance, you've committed yourself to the maximum price, which any smart buyer will begin to chip away. You've put yourself in a defensive bargaining position. That's not where you want to be.

The Merely Bad Opening Move

Buyer: "How much do you want for the property?"

You: "I haven't made up my mind. How much are you willing to pay?"

Now you've put the burden on the buyer, which is good because she may come in with a higher price than you intended. But your reply is too general and it's unlikely she will take the bait and open up with a dollar figure. She will probably fish around for details, then ask you again to name your figure.

The Good Opening Move

Buyer: "How much do you want for the property?"

You: "Please, make me an offer."

Now you're cooking! You've put the burden entirely on the buyer. If she tries to wiggle out, tactfully repeat your position. "Please, make me an offer." In most cases, if the buyer is really interested, you'll get one. If it's not what you want to hear, you can start bargaining up from there.

The Use of Counteroffers

Once you've heard your opponent's offer, counteroffers serve a number of important functions that can help you get what you want:

➤ They keep the bargaining alive and breathing when you seriously want to do the deal. You can reject your opponent's offers without making counteroffers of your own, but your opponent will most likely just walk away from the deal. So if you want to make a deal, the best approach is to make a counteroffer.

Dealmaking Tip
When you receive an offer or counteroffer that you can't accept, one of your first thoughts should be: Should I make a counteroffer?

➤ They demonstrate how serious you are about the bargaining and how you are trying to reach a mutually favorable agreement. By making a counteroffer you show that you're not just stringing your opponent along or rejecting every proposal you don't like.

➤ They place your terms and conditions under a magnifying glass. Your opponent may not have thought of some of your suggestions or compromises. She may even like them.

Guidelines for Making Offers and Counteroffers

There are some important rules you should remember when you start to make offers and counteroffers:

Dealbreaker Alert
People frequently try to back out on deals for a variety of reasons, ranging from getting cold feet to making a better deal with someone else. As soon as you get to the offer stage, start a paper trail so you can prove your opponent has made a commitment to you.

➤ *Never appear too anxious.* Your eagerness may suggest that you desperately want to cut a deal. Your opponent will smell your fear and drive a harder bargain.

➤ *Be prepared for any reaction from your opponent.* From "Whadda you, crazy? I wouldn't pay ten cents for that pit you call a house!" to "How does three million sound?" Don't be caught off-guard, even if your opponent's reaction isn't what you expected.

➤ *Always get offers and counteroffers in writing.* If you negotiate a good deal and your opponent tries to back out, you've got a written record to prove that you had already reached an agreement.

➤ *Be specific when you state your offers and counter-offers.* "I'll give you three thousand dollars" is better than "I'm thinking somewhere in the area of three thousand dollars." The vague approach invites your opponent to try for more.

➤ *Explain the reasons for your offers and counteroffers.* Say you're interested in buying a used car that's going for $10,000. You have the car checked out and discover that it needs $1,000 worth of repairs. You should pass that information on to your opponent when you make a $9,000 counteroffer. That makes it clear to your opponent that you have a legitimate reason for offering $9,000—you're not just trying to chisel away at his price.

> **Dealbreaker Alert**
> Your bargaining will be difficult if your opponent is suspicious of your motives. If you make offers or counteroffers with no explanation, you force your opponent to guess what you're up to. Usually, your opponent will imagine the worst. That makes it unlikely your offer or counteroffer will be accepted.

➤ *Don't get angry if your offer or counteroffer is rejected.* You don't want to offend your opponent. Ask him why he's rejecting your offer—perhaps he has legitimate reasons that you can equalize.

Why Highballs and Lowballs Are for Screwballs

Making outrageously highball or lowball offers is a foolish bargaining strategy. If your price is too high (if you're the seller), or too low (if you're the buyer), you risk losing your credibility unless you can give your opponent some reason for your position. That credibility damage will spill over onto every bargaining position you take.

If you negotiate regularly, and you develop a reputation for coming in with highballs or lowballs, many of your opponents will automatically discount your proposals, no matter what they are. That's much too heavy a price to pay for those few situations when you might get an inexperienced opponent to swallow a highball or lowball offer.

> **Let's Talk Terms**
> *Highballing*: Naming a figure or term that is much too high for the negotiation.
>
> *Lowballing*: Naming a figure or term that is much too low for the negotiation.

165

What to Do When Your Opponent Throws You a Highball or Lowball

When your opponent makes offers or counteroffers that you know are too high or too low, ask for an explanation. Maybe your opponent is misinformed or just made a mistake.

If your opponent is deliberately coming in too high or too low, requesting an explanation will call your opponent's bluff. That puts your opponent on the defensive and swings the bargaining momentum to you.

How to Treat Your Opponent's Offers or Counteroffers

Always look at your opponent's suggestions objectively, even if they're obviously too high or too low. If you're not happy with your opponent's offers or counteroffers, explain why. That puts your opponent on the defensive.

Be gentle when you reject an offer or counteroffer. Remember, your opponent has a lot of her "self" invested in her offer or counteroffer. If you don't explain why you can't accept the offer or counteroffer, you run the risk of offending her.

Dealmaking Tip
I explained in Chapter 7 why you should set deadlines when you bargain. Be sure you set a deadline for any offer or counteroffer you make. Make deadlines your bargaining ally.

If you like your opponent's offer or counteroffer, don't tip your hand! If you appear too pleased (by grinning like an idiot, singing a merry song, or leaping up and performing a victory dance on the table), your opponent will have second thoughts on the wisdom of her offer or counteroffer and may withdraw it. So keep a level, calm, and passive attitude. Tell your opponent you'll get back to her within the deadline period (if one has been set) or very soon. Or, you can accept on the spot if you feel it's the right thing to do.

Identifying Dealmakers and Dealbreakers

Many negotiators talk about throwing dealmakers or dealbreakers into the negotiation at the offer or counteroffer stage.

A *dealmaker* is anything that's thrown onto the bargaining table that clinches the deal. For example, say that you are negotiating to buy a house and you and the seller have agreed on all the details, but you're still $5,000 apart on the price. Then you offer to split the difference and spend the $2,500 more on the house. The seller, finally pleased with all the terms of the deal, accepts. Your split-the-difference suggestion was the dealmaker.

A *dealbreaker* is the opposite of a dealmaker. It's anything thrown onto the bargaining table that kills the deal. With the home-buying example, say that when you offer to split the $5,000 difference, the seller refuses and insists that you pay the entire amount. If you walk away from the deal at that point, then the seller's insistence on the $5,000 was the dealbreaker.

The Legalese of Offers and Counteroffers: A Cautionary Tale

Here's the scenario. You want to buy a house. The sellers—remember Joe and Jane Jones?—are asking $200,000. You make a counteroffer for $150,000 and add the following conditions:

➤ The Joneses' lawnmower comes with the deal.

➤ The large doghouse comes with the deal. (Fido will love it.)

➤ The Joneses will pay for a water-quality test. (You're very health conscious.)

➤ Three living-room chairs come with the deal, and furthermore, the Joneses will re-upholster them in that precious blue chintz pattern you saw in *Martha Stewart Living*. (I know, I know…that's a ridiculous condition. But I've included it to better illustrate the way the law treats offers and counteroffers. Work with me here.)

The Joneses are intrigued but not yet convinced. They make another counteroffer: they will accept all your conditions except the price and the absurd upholstery job. They will sell for $190,000 and will have nothing to do with chintz.

You decide to make a counteroffer. You raise the price to $160,000 and propose that they reupholster only two of the chairs.

The Joneses smell a deal, so they aren't going to walk away yet. They propose splitting the price difference at $175,000. They still refuse to reupholster the chairs.

You want that house. So you make a counteroffer. You accept the $175,000 compromise price but insist on getting at least one chair reupholstered.

And the verdict is…you goofed!!! By insisting on that one chair, you modified the seller's counteroffer and thus rejected the counteroffer. The seller can now reject the entire deal on the basis of that one chair. What if, for example, after you make your counteroffer, someone else comes along and offers the Joneses $175,000 with no stipulations about the reupholstery of the chair? The Joneses can accept that offer and kiss yours good-bye.

Dealbreaker Alert

Any time you alter an offer or counteroffer, you reject the offer—no matter how tiny your alteration may seem. So think carefully about any alterations you suggest, especially if you are close to sealing the deal.

The rule is: Any alteration of an offer or counteroffer, no matter how trivial, is a rejection of the *entire* offer or counteroffer.

You can't accept an offer in little bits and pieces until you have a deal. It's an all-or-nothing game. The same rule applies to your opponent. In that way, the law tries to treat both sides equally and fairly.

In negotiations in which more than one issue is involved, agreements must be reached on all issues, or there's no deal. Tentative agreements in multi-issue negotiations are not binding (unless the parties involved agree to accept tentative agreements before the negotiation has begun).

The Devastating Effects of Making the First Large Concession

Just as you shouldn't make the first offer, you shouldn't make the first large bargaining concession. That will make you appear weak in your opponent's eyes and can destroy your bargaining power.

Dealbreaker Alert

If you have to make the first large concession, make sure you can provide a clear and convincing reason for making it.

The first thing you can do to avoid making a large concession is to make sure all of your negotiating positions are fully supported by facts and documentation. That puts the burden on you to prepare for the negotiation. Head back to Chapter 2 if you need a refresher course in doing your homework.

If your opponent still demands a large concession, ask why. If he comes up with a legitimate reason that you hadn't thought of, you have a genuine basis for making the concession and your concession probably won't cost you your credibility (although you do risk looking unprepared for the negotiation).

If your opponent can't come up with a legitimate reason, you should re-explain the basis for your position. In most cases, if your opponent has any interest in making a deal, he will drop the demand for a large initial concession.

The Least You Need to Know

➤ Always wait for your opponent to make the first offer.

➤ Use counteroffers to keep the negotiation alive and to indicate your serious interest in the negotiation.

➤ Get any offers or counteroffers in writing.

➤ Don't use highballing or lowballing strategies. They risk your credibility and make your opponent suspicious.

➤ A counteroffer that alters an offer or counteroffer in any way is a rejection of the entire offer or counteroffer.

➤ Always explain your reasons for proposing or rejecting an offer or counteroffer.

➤ Never make the first large bargaining concession.

Chapter 22

Closing the Negotiation

In This Chapter

➤ When to close the bargaining

➤ Closing do's and don'ts

➤ Closing techniques

Congratulations! You finally made it. You prepared thoroughly, negotiated ferociously, skillfully maneuvered through the offers and counteroffers. Both you and your opponent are ready to say "yes!" The final step is closing the deal. In this chapter, I show you how to successfully conclude a bargaining session well done.

When Is Closing Time?

No two negotiations are alike, so it's impossible for me to predict the perfect time for closing that will work in every negotiation. The key question you should ask yourself is: Do I think my opponent will say "yes"? If you're sure, then you might, for example, shake hands and say, "Okay, it's a deal."

If you're unsure if the time is right, continue the bargaining, perhaps by re-explaining your last counteroffer, or by asking your opponent for more details on her offer or counteroffer. The more bargaining experience you gain, the easier you'll be able to pinpoint the best time to close.

When Your Opponent's Body Language Tells You Not to Close

Back in Chapter 6, I gave you a basic primer on body language and how to interpret it. When you approach closing, observing your opponent pays great dividends. You want to stay alert and notice your opponent's body movements to help you gauge whether the time is right for you to close the bargaining.

Certain gestures or movements suggest that your opponent is not yet ready to say "yes." When you see one or more of the following signs, hold off the closing until you get your opponent in a more receptive mood:

➤ Arms folded tightly against the chest. This is a classic defensive position. Your opponent is subconsciously telling you that he is not ready to say "yes."

➤ Turning his body slightly sideways, even while facing and looking at you. By presenting the side of his body to you, rather than openly facing you, your opponent is protecting himself from fully accepting your bargaining position.

➤ Looking away, even though his body is facing you. If your opponent can't look you in the face, he's not ready to agree to your terms.

➤ Crossing his legs and leaning back, away from you. Your opponent is putting distance between the two of you. He is resisting.

➤ Rising from her chair and moving away from you. Here again, your opponent is trying to distance herself from you.

➤ Rubbing or shielding her chin or face. By putting her hands in front of her face, your opponent is shielding herself because she's having doubts about the negotiation.

If you see one or more of these postures, you know your opponent is subconsciously not ready to commit to closing the negotiation just yet—regardless of what he is actually saying to you. Keep pointing out the worth and value of your proposals until he stops using defensive, shielding postures. Then, and only then, will he be receptive to saying "yes."

What to Expect at a Closing

Most informal negotiations, such as resolving family matters or buying small items of personal property, don't require any ceremonial closing agreements—a simple verbal assent will do.

Other types of negotiations, such as buying or selling real estate, do require extensive closing arrangements. I cover the details of particular closing procedures in Part 7; for now, here are a few pointers to keep in mind at any closing in which you have to sign on the dotted line:

➤ Use a lawyer if you can afford one. Real estate and lease agreements are usually long-term and involve a lot of money. You should be sure you are signing something you can live with. It's better to be safe than sorry.

➤ Always read the document you are asked to sign, clause by clause, and seek an explanation for anything that's not clear. Don't worry about seeming naive or foolish. There's nothing more naive or foolish than signing a document you don't fully understand.

➤ Documents prepared by your opponent are usually loaded with provisions that heavily favor your opponent. It's always better to prepare (or have your lawyer prepare) the document and submit it to your opponent, if that's possible. That way you can insert provisions that are favorable to you.

➤ In most cases, each party should receive a signed original of the closing document or contract. Keep your original in a safe place.

Closing Do's and Don'ts

I've discussed several of the pointers here in previous chapters, but they're important enough to mention again:

➤ DO make good eye contact when you make your closing pitch. That tells your opponent that you believe in the deal. Looking away conveys the impression that you lack confidence in the deal, and your opponent may refuse to go along.

➤ DO use the magic words "fair and reasonable." You want your opponent to know that a truly fair and reasonable person would seal the deal.

➤ DON'T be too anxious to close. If you appear too eager to get your opponent to say "yes," your opponent may get suspicious of you and ask for more time to reexamine the deal.

➤ DON'T beg and plead with your opponent—this will also make you appear anxious. Stay calm and repeat the merits of your position. At some point, your opponent will concede.

➤ DON'T try to bully your opponent into saying "yes." The more you bully, the more your opponent will resist. You'll also risk making your opponent angry.

Four Words That Can Devastate a Closing

I once watched a negotiator bring a long, arduous negotiation to a spellbinding close. He presented his case beautifully, deftly navigated the offer and counteroffer stage, and remained respectful and pleasant throughout. He had his opponent ready and willing to say "yes."

Then he made a cardinal bargaining mistake. He said, "Please, think it over." With those four words, he lost a golden opportunity to get what he wanted. He gave his opponent an open invitation to rethink his bargaining position, and aim for ways to improve it. And that's exactly what his opponent did—he came back to the bargaining table with new ideas and new proposals.

When you give your opponent time to think over a negotiation that is about to close, you offer her time to regroup, to rethink her bargaining position, and to concoct new positions she lost sight of during the negotiation. When she comes back to the bargaining table, she'll be eager to present her new positions—not to say "yes."

Dealbreaker Alert

Never give your opponent a second chance to reconsider anything that's resolved. Your goal is to funnel the bargaining so closed matters stay closed. When you allow your opponent the luxury of thinking things over, you're handing her an invitation to reopen the bargaining.

The moral is, when you sense your opponent is ripe for saying "yes," make the deal right there and then.

Effective Closing Techniques

A closing technique is a cue to get your opponent to say "yes." It's not a device to trick your opponent to say "yes" if he isn't ready. If your opponent isn't ripe to say "yes" when you use a closing technique, no amount of skill will succeed in getting your opponent to close the deal.

Use the following techniques when the issues have been thoroughly discussed and you sense your opponent is ready to say "yes" to the deal. These techniques will get your opponent off the fence and ready to agree to a deal.

Prompting Action Technique

You can encourage and motivate your opponent to say "yes" by asking her to take some simple form of action which signifies that you have a deal. For example, you hand her the closing papers and say, "Please sign here." Or you can simply ask, "Does this mean we have a deal?" In either case, you are suggesting your opponent take an action—sign a paper, or verbally commit to an agreement—that will prompt the closing of the deal.

Good television commercials use this technique. They'll end with the overenthusiastic announcer yelling, "Order now!" or "Call now!" Same with direct-mail campaigns that ask you to fill out a quick survey or try a free sample issue of a magazine. They're encouraging you to act, to say "yes" to their product. That's exactly what the Prompting Action Technique is designed to do—motivate your opponent to say "yes" and close the deal.

Assumption Technique

Here, you assume your opponent will say "yes," so you prompt the closing action. "I'll call the bank and ask them to go ahead with the loan" or "I'll call the title company and ask them to check out the title to the property" are examples of this closing technique. If your opponent is in a "yes" mood, he will nod or say OK.

Summarizing Technique

What you do is *briefly* summarize your understanding of the deal to prompt your opponent to say "yes" to it in its entirety.

When you use this technique, your goal is to reaffirm issues that you've both already decided. You don't want to open up old issues for further discussion. To avoid this, phrase your summation in positive sentences rather than questions, and never use this technique if your opponent hasn't agreed to any of the points you plan to mention in your summation.

Say you're working with Smithers from Wonder Widgets to close a special deal. You summarize the discussion by saying, "So we're looking at a rush order of 5,000 widgets with the company logo engraved on the handle. They'll be delivered to the Chicago office on the 28th, and the price is 50 cents per widget." To which Smithers agrees.

The Final Word on Closing

Once your opponent says "yes" and the details have been wrapped up, don't discuss anything related to the bargaining. You don't want to run the risk of reopening discussions. Make small talk about the weather, sports, the news, your Aunt Edna's kidney stones—anything that's not connected with the subject matter. When your opponent has said "yes," STOP.

The Least You Need to Know

➤ Close the bargaining when you sense from your gut instinct and your opponent's body language that your opponent is ready to say "yes."

➤ Make sure you have all the necessary paperwork, correctly prepared, ready for the closing.

➤ Don't bully or plead with your opponent to close.

➤ When you sense your opponent is ready to say "yes," close. Never ask your opponent to think it over.

➤ Use closing techniques to prompt your opponent to act.

➤ Once you and your opponent have agreed on a deal, don't continue to discuss the deal. You risk reopening the bargaining if you do.

Part 7
Everyday Negotiating Situations

Now let's look at how to negotiate everyday matters you'll deal with many times as you wind your way through the trail of life. Buying a home, car, or real estate; asking for a raise, loan, or refund—many people dread these common negotiating situations. But not you! Once you know how to negotiate them smoothly and powerfully, you'll be able to save a lot of time, money, and trouble. And with the knowledge I pass on to you in this part, you'll not only lose your fear, you'll actually come to enjoy the process.

Chapter 23

Negotiating to Buy or Sell a Home

In This Chapter

➤ The role of agents and brokers in buying and selling a home

➤ The most important information you need when you buy a home

➤ Making offers and counteroffers

➤ What to expect at the closing

Whether you want to live in a grand Victorian mansion or a small bungalow, most of you probably envision yourselves owning a home at some point in your life (if you don't already). It's a cherished part of the American dream—and will continue to be, despite the soaring costs of home ownership.

When you buy or sell a home, there are certain basic pointers you should follow to get the best deal. When you use them, you'll find it's not that hard to get the deal you want. In this chapter, I show you how to conduct a hassle-free negotiation when you buy or sell a home.

Some of the material presented here was adapted from *The Complete Idiot's Guide to Buying & Selling a Home* by Shelley O'Hara. It's a great resource for home buyers or sellers.

The Players in the Real Estate Game

Once you jump into the market to buy or sell a home, any number of real estate experts will offer their services. Here are the key players you may deal with:

➤ *Brokers* are licensed to sell real estate in their state (and can be licensed to sell it in other states). Brokers usually are agents of (work for) the seller, and they charge the seller a commission (usually a percentage of the sales price). The amount of the commission is negotiable and is decided when the seller agrees to hire the broker. Brokers can also open their own real estate offices.

➤ *Salespeople* or *sales associates* are licensed to sell real estate in their state. They cannot open their own real estate offices or conduct business on their own. They must work for a broker. They also are agents of the seller.

Do You Need an Agent?

For both buyers and sellers, agents can help define your search and serve as your representatives to the other side. Agents can help with:

➤ *Financing.* Agents can analyze your current financial situation, estimate the costs involved with a home you are interested in buying, or help you set the listing price on the home you are selling.

➤ *Finding a home.* If you aren't sure what kind of home you'd like to buy, an agent can help define your terms. She will have information about communities, schools, taxes, and neighborhoods. She will also arrange all your visits to homes and will tour them with you.

➤ *Preparing your home.* Agents have a good idea what home buyers look for. If you are selling your home, your agent can often tell you which repairs and renovations will increase its sales value and eye appeal.

➤ *Negotiating.* Home buying and selling is an intricate deal with plenty of concessions and fine print. Even though you're a negotiating whiz because you've read this book, you may still want an agent to represent you at the bargaining table.

If you are selling a home, I'd say you almost definitely need an agent. Some home sellers, though, choose to go it alone.

For Sale by Owner: Selling Your Home On Your Own

If you want to sell your home by yourself, you'll have to become an instant expert in a number of professions. You'll need to be a canny advertiser, an enthusiastic seller, a market researcher, a shrewd financier, and a master negotiator. I can help you with that last part, but as for the rest, you're on your own.

You will also have to be "on call" any time someone wants to see your place. You probably won't have the luxury of showing it only on evenings and weekends.

The Downsides of Dealing With Agents

For one, agents cost money. Buyer's agents usually get a flat fee or a commission based on the purchase price of the home. Seller's agents usually get a five- to seven-percent commission of the selling price. (Commissions are negotiable, too.)

Remember that because agents usually represent the seller on a commission arrangement, they will desperately want to push the deal through.

If you're the buyer, you can offer less than the listed (or asking) price and, in many cases (unless the house is a hot property with a lot of interested buyers) you'll get the house for a reasonable price. That's because the agent will want to make a commission, and will recommend that the seller accept any reasonable offer.

On the other hand, if you're the seller, you have to prevent your agent from pushing for a sale that's lower than your asking price. The time to do that is when you list the price with the agent. Make it clear to the agent at that time that you'll stand firm on the listed price unless a buyer comes up with a genuine reason why you should take less. (If you sell your house yourself, of course, none of this applies.)

Let's Talk Terms
In many states, the *listed* or *asking* price is considered the seller's offer for the house.

What to Look for When You Buy a Home

There are literally hundreds of factors you should consider when you evaluate a home: the size, the style, the maintenance, the property, the neighborhood, and the school district, to name a few.

In terms of negotiation, though, there are a few specific factors you should investigate once you've found a house you like.

Nobody Wants It

You should find out how long the house has been on the market. If the "For Sale" sign has been up for a while, the house may have defects, or the neighborhood may be changing for the worse.

On the other hand, perhaps the house is fine but the asking price is too high. Frequently, homes that are sold by their owners stay on the market longer because owners tend to price their homes too high—they are emotionally attached to their home and may be unable to set an unbiased price, or they may be inexperienced sellers.

It's a Buyer's Market

While a good seller (or agent) won't disclose how anxious the seller is to make the sale, you may be able to gauge his desperation level from a few key facts:

➤ How long the house has been on the market. If it was just put on, chances are the seller isn't particularly anxious. If it's been on a while, he may be more than ready to make a deal.

➤ Whether the selling price has been reduced, and if it has, how many times.

➤ The personal situation of the owner. Has he already bought another house? Is he getting divorced or transferred?

On occasion, an agent may advertise, "Must sell. Owner transferred," or something similar. If you see a listing like that, first make sure that the owner really *is* being transferred. Some unscrupulous agents advertise false information just to make the house seem like a better deal. To be sure the information is true, ask the agent for specific details about the transfer: who the seller's employer is, where the seller is being transferred to and when. A legitimate agent will fill you in.

If the information is legitimate, you can usually make a much lower offer than the selling price.

It's a Money Pit

When you first view a house, it's easy to be swayed by appearances like a well-kept garden or new deck (or, to the opposite extreme, by peeling paint or five trashed autos sitting in the yard). But what really counts is the infrastructure—the pipes, wiring, heating system, and foundation.

You can ask questions about the house yourself. Sellers are, in many states, required by law to disclose any problems with their home. But you should also arrange to have a professional inspection done. (You can make the deal contingent upon receiving a relatively clean bill of health from the inspector.)

Should you discover any large faults with the house, such as an unstable roof or an antiquated heating system, you may be able to deduct the repair costs from the selling price of the house. Or the seller may agree to arrange and oversee the repairs for you.

But you can only do this for large, necessary repairs—don't nit-pick. (Wanting to re-cover the toilet seat in fake fur does not qualify as a necessary expense.) If the seller gets the impression that you are hung up on petty details, she will get angry and that will make any further negotiation difficult.

Terms Every Home Buyer Should Know

So you've found the perfect home. What kind of issues can you negotiate? You may think only about the selling price, but in fact there are many other conditions you may want to specify in the deal:

➤ *What else the seller will pay for.* Closing costs, inspection, appraisal, title search, and document fees are some costs you can ask the seller to pick up.

➤ *Contingencies (what has to happen for the deal to close).* You can make the deal contingent upon getting financing, a clear deed and title for the house, a professional inspection, a professional appraisal, or other hurdles that must be cleared before you sign the deal.

➤ *Deadlines.* When you must have a response to your offer, and when the seller must be out of the house.

➤ *Extras.* What else comes with the house: appliances, furniture, fluffy dog, cookies baking in the oven (just kidding about those last two).

➤ *Condition of the house.* If the seller agrees to any necessary repairs, you will want them completed before you move in.

Making the Offer

Once you've decided on your terms, you must include them in a written (not verbal) offer form, sometimes referred to as a "purchase agreement." A sample purchase agreement is shown later in this chapter. You can draw up (or have an agent or lawyer draw up) your own offer form, but that isn't recommended. It's time-consuming, and there's a good chance you might forget something important.

Most states have written offer forms that you can get from agents, your local real estate association, or from stationery or office supply stores. Use a form. It's easier and safer.

Your offer form should include the following information:

➤ The address and legal description of the property

➤ The price, down payment (often called "earnest money"), and when and how the balance will be paid

➤ A time limit for response to your offer (see Chapter 7 for more on setting deadlines)

➤ The conditions and contingencies that must be met before the deal is finalized— getting a loan, making any repairs or improvements to the house, having the house inspected, and so on

➤ Who pays the property taxes as the deal is in process

➤ When the closing shall take place if the counteroffer is accepted

What Should Your Offer Be?

There are several kind of offers you can make in relation to the asking price:

➤ *The lowball.* As I said in Chapter 21, I'm not fond of lowball offers, and I don't recommend them. If you must, make one only if you are not completely committed to the house.

➤ *The highball.* If you are anxious to seal the deal, you can make your first offer your best offer. But never make it higher than the seller's asking price, unless another buyer has already offered that price and you want to top it.

➤ *The bidding war offer.* If other buyers are interested, you'll have to bid for the house like you'd bid on a hand of poker. If you can't see and raise an offer, you'll have to fold.

➤ *The negotiable offer.* This is the one that leaves room for wheeling and dealing. It's usually the best approach and the one that can lead to the greatest savings.

Making Concessions

Unless your deal is accepted or rejected on the spot, your offer will probably be met with a counteroffer from the sellers. A sample counteroffer form is shown later in this chapter.

Dealbreaker Alert
Try not to get too attached to any house you look at. If you do, you make yourself vulnerable to emotional manipulation and may make a bad deal. As disappointing as it is to lose a deal on a house you like, remind yourself that there is no one perfect house for you. If you stay in the market long enough, you'll find several houses that you like.

At this point, you can accept or reject the counteroffer, or respond with yet another counteroffer. A few pointers to keep in mind as you maneuver through the offer-counteroffer stage:

➤ Small financial concessions can equal a lot of money. If you can chip away at even $1,000 on the sales price, you can save over $2,642.40 (assuming you finance the house with a 30-year, eight-percent interest loan).

➤ If you find yourself making many changes to a counteroffer, you may want to draw up an entirely new form. A marked-up original covered with crossed-off and written-in items points out all too clearly how many concessions you are asking for. A clean copy may be psychologically easier for the sellers to sign.

➤ Don't agree to any verbal offers. Get everything in writing.

➤ Don't split hairs. Remember, you are there to get a house, not pummel the sellers into submission. Wherever possible, look for "win-win" solutions to all your disagreements. You'll make better progress if the sellers feel comfortable with the deal.

➤ If you don't like a counteroffer, or a contingency isn't met, you're free to walk away from the deal.

GRAVES REALTORS®

Selling Broker *Graves Realtors* (# *Grav 8*) By *Maria Bluester* (# *251*)
Listing Broker *Otan Real Estate Co* (# *OTRE 1*) By *Charles Chuck* (# *127*)

PURCHASE AGREEMENT

1. Date: *July 12, 1994*
2. Buyer offers to buy real estate (the "Property") known as *3569 Camelot Lane*
3. in *Clay* Township, *Hamilton* County, *Carmel* Indiana *46033* Zip Code, which is
4. legally described as: *Lot 23 Brookstone Village, Section 2*
5. in accordance with the terms and conditions set forth below:
6. **A. PURCHASE PRICE:** Buyer agrees to pay $ *103,000—* for above Property.
7. **B. IMPROVEMENTS AND FIXTURES:** The above price includes all improvements permanently installed and affixed, such as, but not limited
8. to, electrical and/or gas fixtures, heating equipment and all attachments thereto, gas grills, incinerators, window shades, curtain, rods,
9. drapery poles and fixtures, awnings, TV antennas, all landscaping, mailbox, garage door opener with control(s), ceiling fans, smoke alarms,
10. mini barns/storage sheds, satellite dish with control(s) and the following:
11. *all items as listed in MLS #418369 also include refrigerator in*
12. *kitchen, fireplace screen and tools*
13.
14. All items sold shall be fully paid for by Seller at time of closing the transaction.
15. **C. METHOD OF PAYMENT:** *(Circle appropriate paragraph number)*
16. 1. **CASH:** The entire purchase price shall be paid in cash and no financing is required.
17. 2. **NEW MORTGAGE:** Completion of this transaction shall be contingent upon the Buyer's ability to obtain a (Conventional) (Insured
18. Conventional) (FHA) (VA) (Other_____) first mortgage loan
19. for $ *90% of sale price*, payable in not less than *30* years, with an original rate of interest not to exceed *9%* %
20. per annum. Buyer shall pay all costs of obtaining financing, except *seller shall pay 2 discount*
21. *points for buyer*
22. 3. **ASSUMPTION:** Buyer shall pay (approximately) (exactly) $_____ in cash and agrees to pay the unpaid balance of
23. the note and to perform the provisions of the existing mortgage on the Property held by_____
24. Seller represents that the unpaid principal balance is [approximately] [exactly] $_____ as of_____
25. 19_____, payable at $_____ per month including interest at a rate of_____% per annum, and also
26. including: (taxes) (insurance) (mortgage insurance). The exact balance including interest shall be computed through day of closing.
27. Buyer shall pay the next payment due after closing. If the existing mortgage cannot be assumed by Buyer at the interest rate shown
28. above, Buyer hereby agrees to accept an interest rate not to exceed_____% per annum and if this is not available, at Buyer's
29. option, this Agreement may be terminated. Seller agrees to pay any shortage in escrow account. Buyer agrees to pay all fees charged
30. by mortgagee for assumption. The parties agree to (reimburse the Seller) (assign at no cost to Buyer) any escrow account balance on
31. day of closing.
32. 4. **CONDITIONAL SALES CONTRACT:** Within_____days after acceptance of this Agreement the parties hereto shall approve
33. the Metropolitan Indianapolis Board of REALTORS' Conditional Sales Contract form or another acceptable form embodying the terms
34. contained herein.
35. Cash down payment $_____, interest rate on the unpaid balance_____% per annum calculated monthly and paid monthly
36. in arrears; monthly principal and interest payment $_____; first payment shall be due on_____, 19_____. In addition
37. interest shall commence the day after closing; Property taxes and insurance are to be paid (separately when due) (monthly) in addition
38. to the monthly principal and interest payment; no prepayment penalty for early pay-off; a_____day default period for any
39. time provisions; forfeiture provisions are to be released by Seller when Buyer has paid more than $_____ or (_____%)
40. of the purchase price. Contract shall be paid in full on or before_____, 19_____.
41. Special provisions:_____
42.
43.
44. The Conditional Sales Contract is to be prepared by_____
45. at_____ expense. Buyer shall only use the Property for_____
46. **D. TIME FOR OBTAINING FINANCING:** Buyer agrees to make application for any financing necessary to complete this transaction, or for
47. approval to assume the unpaid balance of the existing mortgage within *5* days after the acceptance of this Purchase
48. Agreement and to make a diligent effort to obtain financing in cooperation with the Broker and Seller. No more than *30* days
49. after the acceptance of the Purchase Agreement shall be allowed for obtaining favorable commitment(s) or mortgage assumption approval.
50. If a commitment or approval is not obtained within the time specified above, this Agreement shall terminate unless an extension of time for
51. this purpose is mutually agreed to in writing.
52. **E. CLOSING DATE:** Closing date shall be on or before *August 15*, 19 *94* or within *3* days
53. after *loan approval*, whichever is later.
54. **F. POSSESSION:** Seller may retain possession of the Property up to 12 o'clock midnight on *August 18*, 19 *94*
55. or 12 o'clock midnight *3* days after closing the transaction, whichever is later, and Seller's possession until that date shall be
56. free of rent. If Seller does not deliver possession by that date, Seller shall pay Buyer $ *100.—* per day as liquidated damages
57. until possession is delivered to Buyer; and Buyer shall have all other legal and equitable remedies available against the Seller.
58. **G. INSPECTIONS:** *(#1 OR #2 MUST BE CIRCLED AND INITIALED)*
59. 1. Buyer reserves the right to have the Property inspected. All inspections shall be made within *10* days after *acceptance*
60. with written reports delivered within SEVEN days thereafter to Buyer, Buyer Agent and/or Sub-Agent and Seller and/or Listing agent.
61. Inspections are to be at Buyer's expense by qualified inspectors or contractors, selected by Buyer.
62. If the Buyer does not make a written response to a report within FIVE days of its receipt, the Property shall be deemed to be acceptable.
63. Inspections include, but are not limited to, heating, cooling, electrical, plumbing, roof, walls, ceilings, floors, foundation, basement, crawl
64. space, well, septic, water analysis, wood eating insect infestation and radon. Other_____
65. If the inspection report reveals a major problem affecting the Property, and the Seller is unable or unwilling to remedy the problem, then
66. this Agreement may be terminated by the Buyer.
67. It is agreed that any Property defect previously disclosed to Buyer, shall not be a basis for cancellation of this Purchase Agreement.
68. Inspections required by FHA, VA or lender do not necessarily eliminate the need for other inspections.
69. 2. BUYER HAS BEEN MADE AWARE THAT INDEPENDENT INSPECTIONS DISCLOSING THE CONDITION OF THE PROPERTY ARE
70. AVAILABLE AND HAS BEEN AFFORDED THE OPPORTUNITY TO REQUIRE AS A CONDITION OF THE AGREEMENT THE ABOVE
71. MENTIONED INSPECTIONS. HOWEVER, BUYER HEREBY WAIVES INSPECTIONS AND RELIES UPON THE CONDITION OF THE
72. PROPERTY BASED UPON BUYER'S OWN EXAMINATION AND RELEASES THE SELLER, BROKER, AND LISTING AGENT,
73. BUYER AGENT AND/OR SUB-AGENT FROM ANY AND ALL LIABILITY RELATING TO ANY DEFECT OR DEFICIENCY AFFECTING
74. THE PROPERTY, WHICH WAIVER SHALL SURVIVE THE CLOSING.
75. **H. REAL ESTATE TAX:** BUYER shall pay all real estate property taxes, beginning with the installment due and payable in
76. *May*, 19 *95*, and SELLER shall pay all real estate property taxes due prior thereto. In the event real
77. estate taxes are unknown at time of closing, then the last installment of such taxes shall be used as a basis for any credits due Buyer. Buyer
78. agrees that any variance between actual tax liability and the amount credited at closing shall be their sole responsibility, and Buyer agrees,
79. if necessary, to escrow an amount necessary to satisfy the first installment of taxes due after closing. ("Real Estate Taxes" shall include all
80. charges placed on Tax Bill for collection.)

1-94/P-200

81. **I.** **TITLE EVIDENCE:** Prior to closing, Buyer shall be furnished at Seller's expense, a commitment for title insurance in the amount of purchase
82. price. Any encumbrances or defects in title must be removed from said commitment and subsequent title insurance policy issued free and
83. clear of said encumbrances and title defects, with the exception of any mortgage assumed by Buyer. The final policy shall be subject only to
84. taxes; easements and restrictive covenants of record, encumbrances of Buyer; and rights or claims of parties in possession, boundary line
85. disputes, overlaps, encroachments and any other matters not shown by the public records which would be disclosed by an accurate survey
86. and inspection of this Property. The commitment shall be ordered (immediately) (after mortgage approval) (other _____
87. _____).

88. **J.** **SETTLEMENT/CLOSING FEE:** If the method of payment for this transaction is cash, assumption, or conditional sales contract, the
89. settlement/closing fee shall be paid by _____

90. **K.** **SURVEY/SURVEYOR LOCATION REPORT:** At Buyer's expense a (staked survey) (improvement location report) of the Property is
91. required, which shall (1) be received prior to closing, (2) be reasonably satisfactory to Buyer, (3) be certified as of a current date, and (4)
92. show the location of all improvements and easements.

93. **L.** **UTILITIES/MUNICIPAL SERVICES:** Seller shall pay for all municipal services and public utility charges through the day of possession.

94. **M.** **PUBLIC IMPROVEMENT ASSESSMENTS:** Seller warrants that Seller has no knowledge of any planned improvements which may result
95. in assessments and that no governmental or private agency has served notice requiring repairs, alterations or corrections of any existing
96. conditions. Public or municipal improvements which are not completed as of the date hereof but which will result in a lien or charge shall be
97. paid by Buyer.

98. **N.** **RISK OF LOSS:** Seller shall be responsible for risk of loss and/or damage to the improvements on the Property until time of closing when
99. title to or an interest in the Property is transferred to the Buyer.

100. **O.** **MAINTENANCE OF PROPERTY:** Seller agrees that maintaining the condition of the Property and related equipment is his responsibility
101. during the period of this Contract and/or until time of possession, whichever is later.

102. **P.** **TIME IS OF THE ESSENCE:** Time periods specified in this Agreement shall expire at midnight on the date stated unless the parties agree
103. in writing to a different date and/or time.

104. **Q.** **EARNEST MONEY:** Buyer submits herewith $ _2,500.00_ as earnest money which shall be applied to the purchase
105. price. Earnest money shall be deposited in the listing REALTOR's Escrow Account, immediately upon acceptance of the Purchase
106. Agreement, and held until time of closing the transaction or termination of this Purchase Agreement. Earnest money shall be returned
107. promptly in the event this offer is not accepted. If this offer is accepted and Buyer shall fail or refuse to close the transaction, without legal
108. cause, the earnest money shall be forfeited by Buyer to Seller as liquidated damages, or Seller may pursue any other legal and equitable
109. remedies. The Broker holding any earnest money is absolved from any responsibility to make payment to the Seller or Buyer, unless the
110. parties enter into a Mutual Release or a Court of competent jurisdiction issues an Order for payment.

111. **R.** **HOMEOWNERS ASSOCIATION/CONDOMINIUM ASSOCIATION:** Documents for a MANDATORY membership association shall be
112. delivered by the Seller to Buyer within _____ days after acceptance of this Agreement. If the Buyer does not make a written response
113. to the documents within _____ days after receipt, the documents shall be deemed acceptable. In the event the Buyer does not accept
114. the provisions in the documents and such provisions cannot be waived, this Agreement may be terminated by the Buyer and the earnest
115. money deposit shall be refunded to Buyer without delay. Any approval of sale required by the Association shall be obtained by the Seller, in
116. writing, within _7_ days after Buyer's approval of the documents.

117. **S.** **MISCELLANEOUS PROVISIONS:** The transaction shall be closed in accordance with the following:
118. 1. Prorations for rent, association dues/assessments, or any other items shall be made and computed through the date of closing.
119. 2. Notwithstanding any other provisions of this Agreement, any inspections and charges, which are required to be made and charged to
120. Buyer or Seller by the lender, FHA, VA, Mortgage Insurer or closing agent, shall be made and charged in accordance with their
121. prevailing rules or regulations and shall supersede any provisions of this Agreement.
122. 3. Conveyance of this Property shall be by general Warranty Deed, or by _____
123. subject to taxes, easements, restrictive covenants and encumbrances of record, unless otherwise agreed to herein.
124. 4. Seller agrees to pay the cost of obtaining all documents necessary to perfect title, so that marketable title can be conveyed.
125. 5. If said title insurance is not available, Buyer shall be furnished, at SELLER'S expense, an abstract of title continued to date, showing a
126. marketable title to said Property in OWNER'S name.
127. 6. The price and terms of financing on a closed sale shall be disseminated to members of the Metropolitan Indianapolis Board of
128. REALTORS', to other Brokers upon request, and shall be published in the MIBOR'S Multiple Listing Service.
129. 7. The Professional Service fee payable to the Listing Broker is the obligation of Seller.
130. 8. Seller represents and warrants that Seller is not a "Foreign Person" (individual or entity) and therefore is not subject to the Foreign
131. Investment In Real Property Tax Act.
132. 9. Any amounts payable by one party to the other, or by one party on behalf of the other party, shall not be payable until this transaction is
133. closed.
134. 10. Buyer hereby discloses to Seller that Buyer is licensed under the Indiana Real Estate Broker and Salesperson Licensing Act and holds
135. License # _____

136. **T.** **FURTHER CONDITIONS:** _This offer is contingent upon the closing of_
137. _purchasers' house, at 1024 Hampton Rd. Indianapolis In_
138. _for which an offer has been accepted and is expected to close_
139. _no later than 8/15/94_
140.

141. **U.** **EXPIRATION AND APPROVAL:** This Purchase Agreement is void if not accepted in writing on or before _12_ (AM) (PM)
142. (Noon) (Midnight) _July 13_ , 19_94_.

143. **V.** **TERMS BINDING:** All terms and conditions are included herein and no verbal agreements shall be binding.

144. **W.** **ACKNOWLEDGEMENTS:** Buyer and Seller acknowledge that each has received agency disclosure forms, have had their agency options
145. explained, and now confirm their respective agency relations. They further acknowledge that they understand and accept agency
146. relationships involved in this transaction. By signature below the parties verify that they understand and approve this Purchase Agreement
147. and acknowledge receipt of a signed copy.

148. This Agreement may be executed simultaneously or in two or more counterparts, each of which shall be deemed an original, but all of which
149. together shall constitute one and the same instrument. Delivery of this document may be accomplished by electronic facsimile reproduction
150. (FAX); if FAX delivery is utilized, the original document shall be promptly executed and/or delivered, if requested.

151. _Paul Pierce_ _7/1/94_ _Paula Pierce_ _7/2/94_
152. **BUYER'S SIGNATURE** DATE **BUYER'S SIGNATURE** DATE
153. _PAUL PIERCE_ _PAULA PIERCE_
154. **PRINTED** **PRINTED**
155. _108-03-4153_ _116-32-6498_
156. **BUYER'S SOCIAL SECURITY # / FEDERAL I.D. #** **BUYER'S SOCIAL SECURITY # / FEDERAL I.D. #**

157. **ACCEPTANCE OF PURCHASE AGREEMENT**
158. The above terms and conditions are accepted this _____ day of _____
159. at _____ (AM) (PM) (Noon) (Midnight). , 19 _____
160.
161. **SELLER'S SIGNATURE** **SELLER'S SIGNATURE**
162.
163. **PRINTED** **PRINTED**
164.
165. **SELLER'S SOCIAL SECURITY # / FEDERAL I.D. #** **SELLER'S SOCIAL SECURITY # / FEDERAL I.D. #**

Approved by and restricted to use by members of the Metropolitan Indianapolis Board Of REALTORS†
This is a legally binding contract. If not understood seek legal advice ©MIBOR 1992 (Form No. 310-01/94)

A sample purchase agreement.

COUNTER OFFER # _1_

_6_ (A.M.) (P.M.) _July 12_ , 19_94_

The undersigned hereby makes the following Counter Offer to a certain Purchase Agreement dated

July 12 , 19_94_ , concerning real property commonly known as _____

3569 Camelot Ln in _Clay_ _____ Township,

Hamilton County, . _Carmel_ , Indiana between:

Harry + Harriet Hamilton as Seller(s) and

Paul and Paula Pierce as Purchaser(s).

(1) _Purchase price to be 106,000._
(2) _Seller to pay purchaser's closing costs not to exceed_
    _$1,000._

All other terms and conditions of the Purchase Agreement and all previous Counter Offers shall remain in effect except as modified by this Counter Offer.

This Counter Offer # _1_ is void if not accepted in writing on or before _____ _6_ (A.M.) (P.M.) (Noon) (Midnight) on _July 13_ , 19 _94_ . This Agreement may be executed simultaneously or in two or more counterparts, each of which shall be deemed an original, but all of which together shall constitute one and the same instrument. Delivery of this document may be accomplished by electronic facsimile reproduction (FAX); if FAX delivery is utilized, the original document shall be promptly executed and/or delivered, if requested.

Harry Hamilton _7/12/94_   _Harriet Hamilton_ _7/12/94_
(Seller) (Purchaser) Signature   Date   (Seller) (Purchaser) Signature   Date

_306-75-1234_   _317-18-1920_
Social Security # / Federal I.D. #   Social Security # / Federal I.D. #

ACCEPTANCE OF COUNTER OFFER # _____

The above Counter Offer # _1_ is hereby accepted at _12_ (A.M.) (P.M.) (Noon) (Midnight) _7/13_ , 19 _94_ . Receipt of a signed copy of this Counter Offer is hereby acknowledged. This Agreement may be executed simultaneously or in two or more counterparts, each of which shall be deemed an original, but all of which together shall constitute one and the same instrument. Delivery of this document may be accomplished by electronic facsimile reproduction (FAX); if FAX delivery is utilized, the original document shall be promptly executed and/or delivered, if requested.

Paul Pierce _7/13/94_   _Paula Pierce_ _7/13/94_
(Seller) (Purchaser) Signature   Date   (Seller) (Purchaser) Signature   Date

_108-03-4153_   _116-32-6498_
Social Security # / Federal I.D. #   Social Security # / Federal I.D. #

Approved by and restricted to use by members of the Metropolitan Indianapolis Board Of REALTORS®.
This is a legally binding contract, if not understood seek legal advice.   ©MIBOR 1992   (Form No. 210-01/92)

A sample counteroffer form.

Signing and Closing the Deal

Once you both agree on an offer or counteroffer and sign it, it is a legally binding document. For this reason, you might want to have a lawyer look over the agreement before you sign.

After you sign, you will have to handle financing, insurance, and the inspection—each of which could be covered in its own *Complete Idiot's Guide*. You should also conduct a final walk-through to make sure the house is in good condition and the seller has done everything he was obligated to do under the agreement. If everything falls into place, you will approach the closing. Here are some issues you'll face on closing day:

➤ Determine who will hold the title to the house (in other words, who will own the house). Will it be you alone, or will you hold the title with your spouse or someone else?

➤ Bring along the money you need to close the deal. (You will know the amount in advance of closing day.) You'll need a cashier's check for the amount.

➤ Bring along a homeowner's policy, one-year prepaid receipt, and any other documentation required by the lender.

➤ Review so many documents you'll feel like the prosecutor at the Watergate hearings. These include lending statements, notes, mortgages, affidavits, deeds, title policy, disclosure statements, IRS forms, compliance agreements, and sanity documents to prove that the process hasn't driven you completely crazy.

After payments have exchanged hands and all the paperwork has been signed, you'll walk out of the closing with the keys to your new kingdom. Congratulations!

For Sellers Only: Evaluating an Offer

Your first decision will be whether to hire an agent or sell the house yourself. (See the section "The Players in the Real Estate Game" earlier in this chapter.) Whatever you choose, you should have a firm idea of what you would like to get for your house, what you are willing to settle for, and what is unacceptable. Keep in mind that these figures may change after you test the market.

Once you've snagged an interested buyer, she will present you with an offer in the form of a purchase agreement (a sample purchase agreement is shown earlier in this chapter). The terms mentioned in the offer are listed in the earlier section "Making the Offer." Ask yourself the following questions as you evaluate the offer:

➤ What price did the buyer offer?

➤ How much of a deposit is the buyer willing to put down? This indicates how serious the buyer is about your house.

➤ What contingencies and terms did the buyer specify?

➤ How much time do you have to consider the offer before you have to respond?

At this point, you can accept the offer, reject it, or make a counteroffer. Remember, if you're selling, financial concessions are the least beneficial to make. If you cut $1,000 off the selling price, you lose that $1,000 *plus* any return you could make from investing it. So suggest concessions on non-financial matters (extras, a different moving date, and so on) if you can. Make financial concessions only when it's absolutely necessary.

Read through the earlier section "Making Concessions" for more information about the offer/counteroffer phase.

No One Wants My House!

Remember, selling a house takes time—sometimes months or even more than a year. If you've waited a suitable time and still aren't getting any offers, you may want to sweeten your terms. Specifically:

➤ Should you lower your asking price?

➤ Are there improvements you should make, or agree to make, as part of the deal?

➤ Are there incentives you can add to make the house or property more attractive?

➤ Should you offer to help interested buyers with financing? (Be especially careful with this one. You must understand all financial terms and understand your liability, should the buyers not be able to hold up their end of the bargain.)

The Least You Need to Know

➤ You may choose to hire an agent to help you negotiate the buying or selling of a home. If you choose to sell your home by yourself, you will be solely responsible for advertising, marketing, negotiating, and closing the deal.

➤ If you're buying a home, find out how long the home has been on the market, the condition of the home, and how anxious the sellers are to make the sale.

➤ Negotiable terms in the buying or selling of a home include the price, contingencies, condition of the house, and extras the seller may include with the house.

➤ If you are interested in a house, make a negotiable offer. Make a highball offer if you desperately want the house. Make a lowball offer only if you are willing to walk away from the house.

➤ Get all offers and counteroffers in writing. Aim for a "win-win" negotiation.

➤ If you're a buyer, shoot for financial concessions. If you're a seller, suggest any concessions other than financial ones.

Chapter 24

Negotiating to Buy or Sell Real Estate

In This Chapter

➤ Similarities between buying a home and buying commercial or investment property

➤ Deciding on an asking price for the property

➤ What you should know about a property before you negotiate

➤ Negotiating tips for buying or selling property

So you want to increase your worldly estates by buying a piece of land, either as a site for your business or as an investment down the road. Buying property, whether for commercial or investment reasons, has a lot in common with buying a home, but with a few notable differences. In this chapter, I show you how to buy the best piece of property at the best price.

Dealing With Commercial or Investment Brokers

A major difference between buying commercial or investment property and buying a home is the price tag. Most commercial or investment properties are more expensive than residential properties (unless you're looking to buy a home like Buckingham Palace).

Let's Talk Terms
Commercial real estate is property used for a business, such as a restaurant or health food store. *Investment real estate* is property you buy and hold on to in the hopes of eventually selling it and making a profit. Some investment property, such as vacant land, doesn't produce income, but you buy it hoping to make a profit when you sell.

Along with that, brokers who sell commercial or investment property usually make higher commissions (anywhere from eight to fifteen percent) than brokers who sell homes.

Because he deals with both higher-priced properties and a higher commission, a commercial or investment property broker has a lot more to lose (than might be the case with residential property) if he can't sell a piece of commercial or investment property. That means that in this market, buyers have the advantage—brokers will usually encourage sellers to accept any reasonable offer in order to make the sale.

Buyer's Market: Figuring Out What a Property Is Worth

Property assessment is a specialized science, particularly when it comes to buying a business or investment property; I could write an entire *Idiot's Guide* on the subject. For now I'll give you a brief overview of how you should think about the process.

Let's Talk Terms
Net rent is the money you get after you've paid all the expenses associated with the property (taxes, insurance, maintenance, loan payments, etc.).

If you're buying property as a place to put up your business, determine the maximum cost you can absorb without lowering your profits or placing your business in jeopardy.

If you're buying investment property, figure out how much profit you expect to make (in the form of rents, for example) compared to how much the building will cost you (in the form of taxes, insurance, or loan payments, for example). Negotiate the asking price until you can realize a rate of return you are comfortable with.

Researching Real Estate

As you prepare to negotiate for commercial or investment property, get as much information as you can about the property. The more you know, the more successful you'll be. Here are some sources you can tap to get information:

➤ The seller or the seller's broker. Ask for profit and loss statements, and information on expenses related to the property (taxes, insurance, and so on). If you are refused any of this information you should probably think twice about investing in the property.

➤ Public records, such as the Register of Deeds (find them at the county building or courthouse in the county in which the real estate is located). You can examine the deed and the history of the property.

➤ Title insurance companies. They will check out the title to the property to be sure it is free from defects, so the title company can insure the title. Defects might include liens (unpaid taxes on the property), or conflicting claims of ownership on the property.

➤ A professional examination of the property. This is a must. Have an appraiser evaluate the plumbing, wiring, heating and cooling systems, roof, and basic structure of the property. The appraiser will advise you of any significant problems, or any repairs the property will need.

➤ A personal examination of the property. Check the place out yourself. Talk to tenants and find out if they are happy there. (You don't want to deal with a mass exodus of tenants after you buy the place.)

➤ Existing leases for all tenants who occupy the property. Check out their rents, what expenses they pay for, and when their leases are up for renewal.

Negotiating for Property

Once you've evaluated a property and have decided to negotiate for it, here are some tips that can help you work out a good deal:

➤ Buyers: List any defects you discovered during your inspection. If the roof leaks or the place needs a paint job, those are factors that justify a lower asking price.

➤ Sellers: Acknowledge and prepare to equalize any defects a potential buyer might notice and mention.

➤ Buyers: Never tell the seller why you want the property. Just offer a general, plausible reason: "I'm shopping around for a good investment," for example. If you tip off the seller that you have an important need or desire to buy the property, you're giving her extra reason to insist on a higher price.

➤ Buyers: The offering or listed price of most property is almost always too high. Don't fall for it. Get an appraisal and decide what you can afford to pay to make the investment a profitable one for you. Then make a counteroffer.

➤ Buyers: Make concessions on small items, if that helps you get the property for the price you want. For example, you can offer to pay for the title insurance or having the property surveyed. Or you might consider taking possession of the property at a date more convenient to the seller. Sellers are often influenced by these concessions.

➤ Sellers: Similarly, you might offer to make small concessions that make the property more attractive to a potential buyer. Consider making certain repairs, or paying particular fees. This may influence an uncertain buyer to go ahead and make a deal.

➤ Buyers: Decide in advance the maximum amount you will pay, and stick to it. But be flexible when you bargain. There's always more than one way to close a deal. For example, if you and the seller are $5,000 apart on the price, you can propose other ways to get your actual cost reduced by $5,000.

➤ Buyers and sellers: Don't rush into the deal. Remember, real estate deals often involve a tremendous financial commitment. Make sure the deal is sound before you commit yourself.

The Least You Need to Know

➤ Use the broker's fear of losing the deal to drive a better bargain for the property. If you're the buyer, aim for a lower price than the asking price. If you're the seller, make it clear to your broker that you will not lower your asking price unless there's a good reason.

➤ If you buy property for business use, figure out the maximum cost of buying the property that your business can absorb.

➤ If you buy investment property, decide how much you want to earn on the money you invest. That sets the maximum price you should pay for the property.

➤ Get as much information as you can about the property *before* you bargain.

➤ If you're the buyer, inspect the property for defects that will lower the price. If you're the seller, be prepared to answer (equalize) the buyer's positions that the buyer contends lower the property's value.

➤ Never accept for the seller's asking or listed price. Always shoot for a lower price.

Chapter 25

Negotiating a Lease or Sublease

In This Chapter

➤ How leases and subleases are different

➤ Negotiable lease terms

➤ Five tips for negotiating leases

You may not be ready to make a commitment to buying a house or a piece of property. If that's the case, renting is the way to go.

Renting has become increasingly popular for a number of reasons. For one, when you rent property, you usually don't have to plunk down a huge payment and take out a loan, as you do when you buy property. For another, it's more flexible—it's easy for renters to pick up and move when they need more space or want to relocate.

So there are several advantages to renting rather than buying. In this chapter, I show you how to negotiate for the best terms when you rent.

Lease or Sublease?

When you rent property or an apartment, you'll usually be asked to sign a document called a *lease* (if you're dealing directly with the property owner or landlord) or a *sublease* (if you're dealing with someone who already rents the property or apartment).

The difference is this: When you sublease property, you have no legal connection (in legalese, this is called "privity of contract") with the property owner. Your only legal connection is with the person who subleased the property to you. If you damage the property, or default on any payments, you have to answer to the sublessor, who in turn has to set things straight with the property owner.

Leases can be assigned rather than subleased. When a lease is assigned, both the person assigning the lease and the person to whom the lease is assigned are liable to the property owner.

Let's Talk Terms

When you sign a lease, you become the *lessee* and the property owner is the *lessor*. The lease determines the rights and responsibilities between you and the property owner.

When you rent property from another renter, you become a *sublessee*. The sublease determines the rights and responsibilities between you and the *sublessor* (the person who leased the property from the property owner). The sublease does not cover your obligations or responsibilities to the actual owner of the property.

You and Your Lease

Whether you lease or sublease, you should have a written contract that covers your rights as a renter. Verbal agreements—however well-intentioned—can and often do break down, and without a written contract, renters can face a long stay in tenant court or even eviction.

Many landlords rely on standard, store-bought leases to which they write in any changes, additions, or deletions. Others may write their own leases. Whatever form your lease takes, it should mention the following provisions:

➤ *Rent.* The biggie. Make sure that both the amount and the method of payment are clearly stated in the lease. Can you mail in a check or do you have to pay cash? What happens if your payment is late?

➤ *Term.* How long will you be leasing? How much notice do you have to give before you end the lease? Do you have any options to continue the lease for another term?

➤ *Deposit.* Many landlords require a security deposit to ensure you don't destroy their property during your stay. When and how will the deposit be refunded? Make sure you get a written receipt of any money you pay up front.

➤ *Condition of the property.* Both you and the owner should agree on the condition of the property at the time you move in, so you aren't blamed for damages you weren't responsible for. Ideally, both of you should tour the property, make notes of any damages or defects, and specify in the lease that those damages are not your fault or responsibility. (Some rental agencies have their own standard forms on which renters are asked to note any damages.) The lease should also specify who is responsible for any improvements or repairs that are needed during your stay.

➤ *Pets.* Usually, if it's not expressly forbidden in the lease, little Fluffy or Fido can move in with you—although some rental agencies charge extra rent or an additional security deposit (or both) to cover any damage your pet might cause. Keep in mind, though, that if your pet constantly barks or menaces your neighbors, you might be in violation of other terms of the lease, which require you to not interfere with the safety and security of other tenants.

➤ *Sublets.* Are you allowed to sublet the property? Some leases expressly forbid subletting; others allow it, but only after potential sublessees have been screened by the landlord.

➤ *Default.* What can the landlord do if you don't comply with any of the terms of the lease? The lease should specify what legal action the landlord will take if you are in default of the lease.

➤ *Breaking the lease.* What if you have to move out before your lease is up? Are you penalized? If so, how much?

The terms I've listed here just cover the basics; you may need to add more provisions to cover special circumstances. Are you allowed to have a waterbed in your apartment? Can you run a tap-dance studio out of your fifth-floor apartment? Does your landlord mind if you cram five roommates into a two-bedroom apartment? Make sure any and all special provisions you need are not forbidden in the lease.

When Renters Rent

If you decide to sublet your place, you are still held accountable for all of the terms in the lease. You are still responsible for the rent, for example. For this reason, you might charge a sublessee more, to make some extra money; or less, if you desperately want someone to cover at least part of the rent while you're gone.

Dealbreaker Alert

If you want to sublease property, read the prime lease and make sure that the sublessor has the right to sublease to you. That's the only way you can be sure you won't get kicked out, should the property owner decide to terminate the prime lease.

So if you sublet your place to Derek Destroyer, who doesn't pay up, converts the apartment into a rehearsal studio for his thrash metal band, and wrecks the place while you're gone, you are still responsible for all the rent money and repairs.

For all these reasons, you should consider drafting your own agreement with a sublessee before you hand him the keys to your castle. And many prime leases state that tenants cannot sublet property without the owner's written permission. This allows the owner to screen all potential sublessees.

Terms to Negotiate in Your Lease

The power you have to negotiate over a lease largely depends on the rental market. Apartment dwellers in smaller cities, for example, can get much better terms than their counterparts in tight markets like New York City. Still, if you have room to maneuver, you might be able to negotiate the following terms:

➤ *Rent.* If the landlord's rent is not regulated by law (as it is in some cities, under certain conditions), you may be able to cut yourself a deal if you promise to sign a longer lease, for example, or plunk down more money up front, or even do odd jobs around the place, like cutting the grass or shoveling snow.

➤ *Condition.* Is the owner willing to make any improvements to the property before you move in? Will the landlord replace the old fridge or paint the place? If the owner does agree to make any improvements, be sure to get those promises included in writing in the lease.

➤ *Dates of occupancy.* Can you move in a few days sooner or later without forfeiting rent? Will you get better terms if you sign a longer lease?

➤ *Options.* Will you be able to renew your lease on the apartment or property? You don't want to set up a cozy apartment, or build up a nice business, and then get kicked out when the lease runs out. Protect yourself by having the right to renew when the lease expires. Here are the option terms I recommend:

For retail space, lease the space for two years with three options to renew for an additional six years (two-year renewal terms for each of your three options). If business is good after the first two years and you need more space, you can shop around without being forced to stay for two more years. You're not locked in. If, on the other hand, you want to stay longer, you can exercise your two-year option.

For residential property, a one-year lease is adequate, especially if you can get a couple of options to renew if you want to stay longer. If you simply can't stand the place, you can kiss it good-bye after your one-year term is up.

Let's Talk Terms
In terms of rental agreements, an *option* is your right to renew a lease. For example, you can lease property for a year with the option to renew for another two years at the end of your first lease. You're not forced to renew, but you can if you want to.

For business property, a two- to five-year initial lease term is good, along with three options to renew. For example, you lease the property for three years with three options to renew, all for three years. At the end of the first three-year term, say you like the place and business is good. You can exercise your first option and stay another three years. You can stay for a total of twelve years, reconsidering your location after every three-year period.

Five Tips for Negotiating for Leases

Again, your negotiating power largely depends on the rental market. But you can increase your odds of renting the space you want by following these tips:

➤ Never rush into a lease. Approach it carefully and neutrally, and remember that there is more than one apartment or property out there that's right for you. When you sign a lease, you're entering a legal contract that obligates you to conform with all of its terms. So don't rush into signing unless you're happy with the deal.

➤ If you are using a rental agent to find a place for you, remember that many rental agents work on commission and will get paid only if they successfully pair you up with a property. That means they are motivated to find you the deal you want. Make it clear that you will walk away if the agent doesn't find you a deal you can live with. The agent may be able to sweeten the deal.

➤ Have a lawyer draw up a lease. If your landlord isn't using a standard lease form, she can either write up her own lease, or have an attorney do it. It's in your favor to have an attorney involved, as most property owners heavily stack the terms of their leases in their favor. When you start the bargaining with a lease drafted by you or your lawyer, you can do the same.

➤ By all means, try to reduce the rent (like you needed an expert to tell you that). Even $50 a month can add up to $600 a year for every year you lease the property. That's money you can pour into improving your apartment or your business.

➤ Emphasize what a good tenant you are (you are, aren't you?). Many property owners have had bad experiences with tenants who were unreliable, difficult to live with, or who damaged the property. The more you impress the owner with your cleanliness, professionalism, reliability, and all-around niceness, the better your chances of negotiating a better deal.

The Least You Need to Know

➤ If you want to rent property, you should have a written lease that states the rent, the term of the lease, the deposit, the condition of the property, subletting arrangements, what happens if you default on the lease, and any other provisions you deem necessary.

➤ If you decide to sublet your property, use a written agreement to protect yourself from any damages or costs incurred by the sublessor.

➤ If you are interested in a sublet, make sure the primary lease permits your sublessor to sublease the property to you.

➤ Lease property for a short period of time, with plenty of options to renew the lease if you want to continue to occupy the property.

➤ Never rush into a lease. Don't sign unless you're happy with the deal.

Negotiating to Buy, Sell, or Lease a Car

Negotiations for a car can range from the relatively casual (selling your old clunker to a neighbor for a little pocket money) to the frantic (listening to a salesperson yammer over a 283Z with all the trimmings). In this chapter, I show you the high points of negotiating for any car, whether it's a new Lexus or an old lemon.

Five Focus Points to Remember When You Shop for a Car

Before you walk into a showroom or scour the classifieds, you should do your homework and know what you're looking for. (See Chapter 2 for a refresher course in preparing for negotiation.) When you buy a car, there are five key areas you should concentrate on:

➤ The gross sales price (including extras).

➤ The trade-in value of your car.

➤ The financial terms if you want to finance the deal.

➤ The warranty. Most new cars are warranted and the details vary from each manufacturer and make and model. Used cars rarely come with a warranty, so if you get one, consider yourself lucky. Make sure all warranties are in writing.

➤ The condition of the car, if it's used.

How to Get the Best Deal from a Dealer

Ever watch car salespeople in action? They run through as many emotions in a single session as an entire theater company in a Shakespearean play. They're hawk-eyed and shark-faced when you first enter the showroom. They're jokey and friendly as they make introductions. They're solicitous and concerned while you look at different models. And they're disgusted and scornful when you finally admit what you're willing to spend. But shopping for a new car doesn't have to be an intimidating experience if you do it right.

Beat the Competition

Once you've found the model you want, present the dealer with the highest price you are willing to spend. If you're buying the car outright, think in terms of the highest price you will pay. If you're financing, set your highest monthly payment.

Dealmaking Tip
The more dealers you can get into the picture, the better your odds of getting a good deal. Each dealer that's competing for your business will experience fear of losing you as a customer.

Let's say you tell the salesperson you'll pay no more than $200 a month for five years. You're not making an offer, you're stating a fact. Now the burden is on the salesperson to juggle the price of the car, your old car's trade-in value (if applicable), and the financial terms in order to come up with an arrangement that meets your price.

Use the same approach with a minimum of two to three dealers. Don't make a deal with any of them on the spot. Give them your name and phone number and ask them to either call or write you with a proposal. And be sure to let all of them know you'll be checking on the competition for a better deal. You want to create fear of loss to motivate the salesperson to give you the best deal.

Let's assume that one dealer meets your $200-a-month ceiling and the other two are close. Inform Dealers 2 and 3 that Dealer 1 has met your terms, and you're going to do business with her unless they can do better. In many cases, they will. And if they don't, you still got the deal you wanted.

Use the Dealer's Language

Car ads are full of bold statements like, "Nobody sells for less" or "We'll beat any deal." If you feel a salesperson isn't living up to those claims, use that language. Quote the exact words. Put the burden on the salesperson to stand by the dealership's claims. That puts pressure on the dealer's reputation, which can motivate the salesperson to give you what you want.

Don't Get Attached to Any Car

For most of us, our cars are part of our "self," so it's easy to get emotionally attached to our wheels. (We even name them and talk to them.) But as you're shopping for a car, do your best not to get emotionally attached to any one make or model. Remember, there will always be other models that can fit your needs. You don't want to seem overeager to the salesperson, who can spot an anxious customer like a shark smells blood in the water. You don't want to be the salesperson's next "victim."

Signing and Closing the Deal

Once you've negotiated the deal you want, you will need to finalize a few particulars before you can drive your car off the lot. They include:

➤ Ordering a registration and license plates. Usually, the salesperson will do this for you.

➤ Deciding in whose name the title will be held.

➤ Providing proof of insurance.

➤ Checking the car title to be sure it's correct.

➤ Knowing how much money you'll need to bring in for a down payment.

➤ Discussing dealer financing with the salesperson, if you are interested. Many dealers and car makers now offer their own financing plans.

Buying a Used Car

The fundamentals of buying a used car are the same as those for buying a new car, with a few additional considerations:

➤ You have much more flexibility in price, because chances are the dealer got a good deal on the car (whether through a trade-in or at a used-car auction). So you can safely assume that the asking price of any used car you're interested in is high; you've got plenty of room to bargain downward.

➤ Have a used car checked by a mechanic *before* you buy. (You can usually have this done for less than $100.) If the mechanic discovers any flaws (bad breaks, transmission problems, rust, and so on) and you still want the car, you can use those flaws to bargain for a lower price. Or you can insist that the dealer or seller repair any problems before you will buy the car.

➤ Warranties are a key consideration when you buy a used car. Some dealers give them; most private sellers don't. Recently, a number of large used car dealerships that do give warranties have sprung up, and this trend will likely grow because the used car market is so good. Make sure any warranties you negotiate are in writing.

➤ Try to get the dealer or seller to put any promises about the car's excellent dependability or fine running condition in writing. Then, if the car proves to be something other than Greased Lightnin', you can use that language against the dealer or seller.

Dealmaking Tip

Whether you're buying or selling a used car, there are two books that list prices for most makes and models. The *N.A.D.A. Used Car Guide* (published quarterly by the National Auto Dealers Association), contains information on cars up to seven years old. There's also the *Blue Book Used Car Guide* (published by Kelley Blue Book Company). Use these books as guidelines to help set your price if you're selling a used car, or to evaluate an asking price if you're buying a used car. You can find both books in your library or bookstore.

Selling a Used Car

It's tough to get a top price when you sell a used car. Most buyers are leery of paying a lot of money because used cars traditionally have a lot of problems.

➤ Be prepared to answer any questions or comments made by prospective buyers, such as how well the car has been maintained and how many miles it gets on a gallon of gas (which you can estimate). If you've kept records of repair work, oil changes, lube jobs, and so on, offer to show them to potential buyers.

➤ Remember, you must equalize every position taken by any prospective buyer to get the price you want.

➤ Be sure your old clunker is cleaned and polished—you want it to have plenty of eye appeal.

Leasing a Car

Car leasing has become increasingly popular. If you're not ready to buy a car outright, you might want to consider a lease. Leasing has a couple of advantages over buying:

➤ The money you have to put up for a loan is small compared to the amount you have to plunk down for a new car.

➤ You have a few nice options when the lease is up—you can drop off the keys and leave (if you have a "closed lease") or you can buy the car for the amount specified in the lease.

➤ If you're using the car for business purposes, you can deduct the lease costs as a business expense.

Negotiating a lease is similar to negotiating to buy a car. Keep these points in mind as you negotiate a lease:

➤ Set an upper ceiling of what you can afford to pay per month. Take that figure to at least two (preferably three) dealers. See if they can meet your monthly ceiling on a make and model you like.

➤ Don't set a ridiculously low monthly payment amount that gives the dealer no room to work with. Be realistic.

➤ Many auto makers (Ford, GM, and Mazda, to name a few) frequently run lease specials that are good deals. Keep your eye out when you watch TV or read the newspapers.

➤ When you negotiate, try to get as many free miles as you can. A good target to shoot for is 15,000 miles each lease year.

➤ Car leases vary from two to five years. I recommend a two- to three-year lease because that's the period most new car warranties cover. Check out the warranty period of the car you're interested in and try to peg the term of the lease to the warranty.

➤ As with all documents, read the lease over carefully. (You might even want to ask the dealer for a blank copy to take home and examine before you sign.) Be sure you understand every lease provision before you sign it.

The Least You Need to Know

➤ When you're shopping for a new or used car, tell the salesperson exactly what you're willing to pay. Let the salesperson come up with a deal that best meets your price and needs.

➤ Always get two or preferably three dealers to bid against each other.

➤ Always have a mechanic check a used car before you buy it. If the car has any problems, use them to drive down the asking price.

➤ When you sell your used car, be prepared to answer any of the buyer's questions or comments about your car.

➤ When you lease a car, use the same approach as buying a car. In addition, get the most free mileage you can and take a lease whose term matches the term of the warranty.

Chapter 27

Negotiating a Raise in Pay

In This Chapter

➤ The best time and place to pop the question

➤ How to get your boss in the right mood

➤ The two major reasons most employees fail to get a raise—and how to avoid them

You're a star employee, the Sultan of Sales, the MVP of marketing. For nearly a year, you've come in at seven and left at nine, knocked yourself out on the Smedley account, and oversaw the development of the world's first aerodynamic widget. It's time you got what you deserved. You'll suggest...no, you'll request...no, you'll *demand* a raise.

I've already touched on many of the tips and techniques that will help you convince your boss to give you a raise. In this chapter, I show you some others.

The Best Time and Place

Given the tightfistedness that's sweeping most companies these days, it's probably up to you to request a meeting with your boss to discuss a raise. That means you have the advantage of picking the best place and time for you. Pick the time of day when you're raring to go. If you're sharpest early in the morning, set the meeting for then. If you don't get cranked up until late afternoon, that's when you want to meet.

The last place you want to bargain with your boss is in his office—his home field. But because he's the boss, you probably won't be able to set the meeting place. If you can, though, try to get him to meet you in your office, or suggest a neutral spot such as a local restaurant or quiet conference room.

Catch Your Boss in the Right Mood

Obviously, you don't want to arrange a meeting a few hours before the Third International Widget Manufacturers Gala Convention is slated to begin. Your boss will be too frazzled to give your request the attention it deserves. He may even resent you for asking at such a bad time.

Try to set your meeting for a time when your boss is in a good mood. Maybe the company's earnings just shot up or a big deal was just completed. Maybe the annual conference is finally over and the entire office is relaxed. Or maybe something personal has happened—he's just come back from vacation, or his son just got married, or he was nominated for an industry award. Anything that puts him in a good mood is a good time because he will be more receptive to your request for a raise.

Make Sure You're in a Good Mood

Your own fabulous accomplishments can also have a large impact on both your boss's mood and your own confidence. Try to hit your boss for a raise when you've just finished an important project. Maybe you finally completed that onerous filing overhaul that no one wanted to do. Or you closed a big deal, or won an important account. Maybe your department just won an award for being the most efficient or most productive.

> **Dealmaking Tip**
> Make good eye contact with your boss when you ask for your raise. If you look down or away at that critical time, your boss will conclude that you lack confidence in yourself and in your belief that you deserve a raise. (See Chapter 6 for more information on body language.)

Don't be reluctant to call the good news to your boss's attention when you open the meeting. ("Just got off the phone with Mr. Smithers. He says he's anxious to get started on that ad campaign. I'm so glad I snagged him for a client.") That makes a nice opening into your raise request and makes it very difficult for your boss to turn you down.

Keep a Compliment File

Starting today, I want you to set up a new file in your already overflowing drawer. Call it your compliment file or anything you like. Use it to stash any and all compliments you receive on your work. That includes:

➤ Thank-you notes from clients or customers

➤ Acknowledgments of a job well done from co-workers

➤ Sales figures on projects you've spearheaded

➤ Impressive reports or charts you've put together

➤ Results from surveys you've overseen

➤ Industry awards or honors

When you finally meet your boss to discuss your raise, take your compliment file with you. Invite your boss to flip through it, or use it to highlight some of your more fabulous accomplishments. Your boss can't be expected to remember how smoothly you handled the infamous Smedley fiasco of a year ago. But your compliment file will jog her memory. Besides that, it's a great confidence booster for you.

Have a Specific Target

If your boss is amenable to the idea of giving you a raise, her next question will most likely be, "What do you have in mind?" You should have a specific goal decided on beforehand. You can express your goal in either dollars or percentages. You might ask, for example, for one hundred dollars more a week, or a dollar more an hour, or a ten-percent annual increase—whatever you feel is reasonable.

How can you determine what's right to ask for? If you fish around, you can find a number of comparative figures that may help you set a goal. Some sources of information:

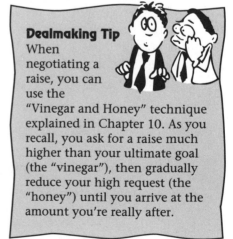

Dealmaking Tip
When negotiating a raise, you can use the "Vinegar and Honey" technique explained in Chapter 10. As you recall, you ask for a raise much higher than your ultimate goal (the "vinegar"), then gradually reduce your high request (the "honey") until you arrive at the amount you're really after.

➤ The *Occupational Outlook Handbook* from the U.S. Department of Commerce offers information on occupational trends and lists average salaries for particular fields and occupations. You can ask for it at your local library.

➤ Industry newsletters and magazines often run salary surveys on particular jobs.

➤ Through the office grapevine, you may be able to discover how much other people in the position you hold (or are seeking) earn.

Why Most People Fail to Get a Raise

The two major reasons most people fail to ask for a raise (besides being lousy at what they do) are fear of losing their jobs and fear of being turned down.

You're Fired—Fear of Job Loss

Usually, the longer you've worked for your employer and the more benefits you have (such as medical and pension benefits), the more attached you'll be to your job and the more you'll fear losing it. Fear of job loss is especially potent in the current tough job market. That's why timing is especially important when it comes to asking for a raise. Don't ask for a raise if:

➤ Your performance hasn't been up to par.

➤ Your company or industry is in a dangerous slump.

➤ Rumors of layoffs or downsizing are wafting through the company corridors.

➤ There have been layoffs or firings in your department.

"Raise? Ha!"—Fear of Failure

Unless you're a billionaire like Bill Gates, you'll also fear getting turned down. That's only natural. And assuming that you haven't been falling asleep on the job, there are a number of legitimate reasons why your boss will tell you no: "There's no money in my budget." "Our company has set salary levels, and you're already at the top of your range." "There's a company-wide wage freeze on."

You can prepare in advance for a "no" by putting together a backup plan that will salvage a bad situation. If your boss says no to a raise, you can suggest other ways to reward your performance:

➤ Performance-based bonus

➤ More vacation time

➤ Flexible working hours

➤ The ability to work at home part-time

➤ Better benefit options

➤ Reimbursement for continuing education

➤ Reimbursement for attendance at a job-related seminar, conference, or workshop

➤ Reimbursement for membership in a professional organization

➤ A promise to reopen salary discussions in a set period of time

You can ward off fear by using mental practice, as I explained in Chapter 15. Visualize yourself talking with your boss. Imagine your boss's response. Run through your reply. Do an entire dress rehearsal several times, in great detail, until you have your approach down pat. You'll find, when you're actually sitting down with your boss, that mental practice has largely eliminated your fears.

The Least You Need to Know

➤ Try to get your boss on your home field (in your office or work area) or, if that's not possible, at a neutral spot.

➤ Pick the time of day when you're sharpest.

➤ Try to catch your boss when he is in a good mood and when your performance has been particularly good.

➤ Be specific on how much of a raise you want.

➤ Think of other benefits you can ask for in the event your boss says he can't give you money but would like to reward your performance.

➤ Mentally rehearse every detail of asking your boss for a raise.

Chapter 28

Negotiating a Loan

> **In This Chapter**
>
> ➤ How to evaluate a lender
>
> ➤ What you can negotiate with a lender
>
> ➤ Information the lender will request from you
>
> ➤ Tips on negotiating with lenders

If you haven't already, sooner or later you'll need to borrow money. Maybe you'll find a dream home, or decide to finally indulge in a new car. Maybe you want to start a new business or go back to school. Whatever your reason, in this chapter, I show you how to negotiate a loan.

Understand Why Lenders Make Loans

Lenders loan you money for one reason—to make a profit. When you borrow from a lender, you must return the money you borrowed *plus* an additional amount—the interest. If lenders don't loan money, they won't make money. So approach any lender with confidence that the lender *wants* to make you a loan.

You should shop around for a lender just like you shop around for a car, house, clothes, and everything else. The competition to loan you money is fierce, so take advantage of it.

If you're shopping for a home loan, check the yellow pages. Lenders are usually listed under "Mortgages." You may also want to check with your bank, other local banks, savings and loans, and credit unions. Many newspapers print a weekly list of lenders and the rates they charge for home loans. There are even lenders who advertise on TV, such as The Money Store. Call several different lenders and arrange to discuss a loan.

Don't be reluctant to visit as many of the lenders as you feel necessary to get a loan arrangement you're happy with.

Choosing a Lender

There isn't enough room here to get into the many complex financial arrangements that lenders are willing to work with. You'll have to do some legwork to decide what kind of loan you want and what kinds are available. For the purposes of this book, though, here's a simple checklist of questions that will help you evaluate a lender:

➤ *What types of loans are offered?* Many large lenders, such as banks, will offer any type of loan you need: business loans, personal loans for vacations or medical bills, educational loans, home-buying loans, and so on.

➤ *What are the payment schedules?* Loan payments can vary in terms of how often you make payments (monthly, quarterly, or biweekly) and how long you have to pay off the loan. These schedules are negotiable and are based on your desires and your ability to pay.

➤ *What is the current interest rate for the type of loan you are interested in?* There's no set interest rate—it depends on your negotiating ability and how much you shop around. If you encounter a lender who quotes you a fixed rate and refuses to negotiate, don't do business with that lender. There are plenty of other lenders who will do business with you.

➤ *What is the prime rate?* You've probably heard the term *prime rate* in the news and have been told that the prime rate is the rate that lenders charge their best customers. Actually, if you have bargaining skills and financial clout, you can probably get a better rate than the prime rate.

➤ *How many points are charged for a particular rate?* Points are a disguised way of saying interest. They are usually associated with real estate loans, especially home loans. The more points you are charged, the higher the cost of the loan—so shop around.

➤ *What fees are charged?* Lenders (again, especially home lenders) charge a variety of fees, such as closing costs, loan application fees, loan processing costs, and similar charges. They all add to the costs of your loan, so get a complete list of the fees before you commit to the loan.

➤ *How long does it take to get the loan?* Each lender has its own processing schedule. Usually it takes from 30 to 60 days to process a loan.

➤ *Are there any penalties on loans that are paid off early?* Some lenders charge prepayment penalties if you pay the loan off before its due date. My advice is to avoid those lenders, because those penalties narrow your borrowing options.

➤ *What is the fee for late payments?* Ask the lender and read the fine print to find out what late charges are assessed. Credit card companies, for example, frequently charge steep penalties for every late payment.

➤ *Who do you deal with if you have a problem or question?* Usually, the person you negotiate the loan with—called the *loan officer*—is the person you contact for more information.

Dealmaking Tip Tactfully let each lender know that you'll be shopping around for the best deal. Lenders usually expect that from customers, and it helps motivate the lender to give you the best deal.

Everything Is Negotiable

When you meet with a loan officer, you'll be able to discuss and negotiate on the following terms:

➤ *The amount of your loan.* Do you want $10,000? $20,000? $100,000?

➤ *The interest rate and points.* Rates can range anywhere from 4 to 15 percent or higher.

➤ *The term of the loan.* How long will you be paying the loan—30 years? 15 years? 1 year?

➤ *The amount of security, if any.* This is how much money you have to put up to secure the loan.

The High Cost of Lending

Before you set your terms, you should explore all your lending options. Small differences in interest rates make a big difference in terms of your wallet. Table 28.1, taken from *The Complete Idiot's Guide to Buying & Selling a Home*, shows you what I mean.

Table 28.1 How Interest Rates Affect Payments

Example 1		Example 2	
Loan Amount	$100,000	Loan Amount	$100,000
Interest Rate	8%	Interest Rate	13%
Term	30	Term	30
Monthly Payment	$733.76	Monthly Payment	$1,106.20

The length of your payment will also affect the amount you need to plunk down every month. Generally, the faster you pay off the loan, the less interest you will pay. Table 28.2 (also taken from *The Complete Idiot's Guide to Buying & Selling a Home*) compares the amount you pay on a 30-year, 15-year, or 30-year biweekly (26 payments a year) loan.

Table 28.2 Comparing Mortgages

	30-Year	15-Year	30-Year Biweekly
Interest Rate	8%	8%	8%
Monthly Payment	$844	$1,099	$422
Principal Paid	115,000	115,000	115,000
Interest Paid	188,779	82,820	135,195
Total Interest Paid	303,779	197,820	250,195

Questions Your Lender Has for You

While you have questions for the lender, the lender will also have questions for you. You should be prepared to reveal the following information and documentation if the lender requests it:

➤ Your current income

➤ Your debt obligations

➤ Your current and past employers

➤ Copies of bank statements

➤ Copies of stock accounts, 401(k), IRA, insurance, and other assets

➤ Copies of pay stubs

➤ W2 forms

➤ Tax returns

➤ Addresses and account numbers for all credit cards and other debts

➤ Explanation and documentation of credit problems, if you have them

➤ Specific information related to the reason for the loan (for example, a copy of a purchase agreement for a loan on a home)

Dealmaking Tip
When you meet with a loan officer, make sure you have all the documentation you need. Being organized and prepared suggests that you are confident you will get the loan (and that you'll be reliable when it comes to paying it back).

Negotiating With a Loan Officer

Let's face it. Negotiating with a loan officer can be scary. Most people are reluctant to discuss their finances with strangers, and many don't have unblemished financial histories.

You don't have to be intimidated about asking for a loan. Most loan officers are fair, reasonable people who want to work with you. Prepare yourself, know what to ask for, act confidently, and remember the following tips:

➤ Prepare for the interview as if it were a job interview. Dress professionally, organize your paperwork, and arrive early.

➤ Make good eye contact with the lender. Lenders prefer confident borrowers because they feel a confident person is more likely to succeed and pay off the loan.

➤ Start the process early. You'll need plenty of time to shop around for a lender. When you find one, you'll need to allow time (usually one to two months) for the loan to go through.

➤ Be truthful about your financial history, even if it isn't unblemished. Explain all credit problems and how you addressed them.

What if You're Rejected For a Loan?

If your loan request is turned down, the loan officer will tell you why. In some cases, you may be able to remedy the situation.

For example, the loan officer may have found that you have a sketchy credit rating (a computerized file of your credit history). Well, there could be a mix-up on your credit report, which you can remedy by calling the credit agencies and asking for a copy of your credit report. (For more on this subject, see *The Complete Idiot's Guide to Managing Your Money*.)

Or maybe you've had some unforeseen expenses—such as steep medical or car repair bills—that have damaged your financial standing. In that case, if you explain and discuss the situation with your loan officer, you can probably still work out a deal on a loan.

If the loan officer is still not convinced, shop around for another lender. Many new loan agencies specialize in lending money to people who traditionally have problems getting loans—people with unfavorable credit histories, for example, or other financial troubles. If you look around, you'll be able to find someone who will give you a loan.

The Least You Need to Know

➤ Shop around for lenders the same way you shop around for a car or house.

➤ Evaluate a lender based on what kind of loan she offers, the terms of the loan, the interest rate, the processing time for the loan, and the fees added to the loan.

➤ Be prepared to give the lender all the information she needs, including current financial status, financial history, and credit, bank, and employer information.

➤ Be sure you understand the amount of down payment, interest rate, and loan term you want.

➤ When you deal with a loan officer, be truthful about your finances, make good eye contact, and dress professionally.

Chapter 29

Negotiating as a Consumer

In This Chapter

➤ What to look for in a warranty

➤ How to ask for a return or refund

➤ What to do if you don't have a receipt or warranty

➤ What to do when you aren't getting good service

If your home is like mine, it's probably packed with appliances and gadgets like vacuums, toasters, CD players, and TV sets—important items that make your life easier and more enjoyable. When these goods break down, it's more than a nuisance to have them fixed or replaced—it's expensive! In this chapter, I show you how to demand, and receive, customer satisfaction.

Check Out the Warranty Before You Buy

A warranty is a promise from the manufacturer that the product you've bought will work as you expect it to work for a certain amount of time. Not all warranties are alike, and some items (which are bought "as is") don't come with warranties at all.

You should check out a company's warranty policy before you plunk down hundreds of dollars on a new computer or stereo system. The warranty should answer the following questions:

➤ How long is the product covered? Two months? One year? A lifetime?

➤ Which parts of the product are covered?

Let's Talk Terms

A *warranty* is a written guarantee by a seller that goods or property will be repaired or replaced if not as represented. In some cases, a purchase may also be protected by an *implied warranty* (one that is not written, but is assumed when you buy the product) or an *express warranty* (an oral or written statement by the seller or the seller's employee). Implied and express warranties are not honored in all cases.

➤ What will the company pay for? Will it pay for replacement parts only, or the cost of repairs on those parts?

➤ What is the repair procedure? Do you have to ship or lug your stereo to the company's repair center? Or will your local retailer cover shipping and handling costs?

➤ How do you begin coverage? With many products, you have to fill out a registration card or customer questionnaire in order to begin coverage. You don't want to find this out the day the product breaks.

➤ What is and is not covered under the warranty? If you try to repair your computer yourself with tape and glue, the company may not be responsible for fixing the damage you've done.

Once you buy a product, you should keep all paperwork related to the purchase—store receipt, credit card slip, warranty, and owner's manual—together in a safe place in your files. I know, I know—this is easier said than done. But a little efficiency up front can save you lots of dough down the road.

Never Pay in Advance!

A word of caution: Whenever you're buying expensive equipment or paying for expensive repairs, try not to pay the entire amount until you're completely satisfied that the product and services are worth the money. Protect yourself by:

➤ Choosing a financing option so you can pay in installments rather than all at once (if you choose to go this route, check the interest rates and late fees).

➤ Paying by credit card, rather than cash or check. Many credit card companies will withhold payment to a particular store if you aren't happy with the product or service.

➤ Placing as small a down payment as possible on repairs or home improvement jobs. By withholding as much money as you can, you give yourself extra bargaining leverage if you're not happy with the work.

Finding the "Yes" Person at the Store

Let's say one fine day, the screen on your computer reads "Out of Order." If you've got a receipt and warranty, your next step is to head back to the store and explain your situation to the person who can give you what you want.

Usually, cashiers and salespeople are not authorized to handle returns or refunds, especially for large items. They may also be too harried to give your request the attention it deserves. If you hold up the line blathering to Suzy Salesperson about how you lost your computerized grocery list file, there's a good chance she will escape to the office of Melissa Manager, do a slipshod job of presenting your case, and then come back and gleefully inform you that Melissa rejected your request for a refund.

To prevent this from happening, you should head for the "yes" person (you remember the "yes" person from Chapter 3, don't you?). Usually, this means the Customer Service Department (most major department stores have these), or, in smaller stores, the manager, assistant manager, or store owner.

Unless you want to be taken for a crank or crackpot, I suggest not storming into the store shouting, "I demand to see the manager!" Instead, politely explain that you've got a refund situation and that you want to speak with the person who is authorized to give you a refund or replacement.

Dealbreaker Alert
Most employees lack the authority to give you satisfaction when your warranty has run out. Insist on dealing directly with the "yes" person—usually, a store manager or owner.

Making Your Case

Once you locate Melissa Manager, greet her cordially and make good eye contact. Tell her how often you and your friends and family shop at her store.

Speak slowly and clearly as you reveal why you're there. I suggest telling your story as a chronological narrative, and presenting any paperwork you have as it becomes relevant:

"I bought this Smarto computer from your store a month ago." (Show the receipt.) "I've been using it to store personal files and browse the Internet—maybe an hour or two a night. Last week, when I went to open a particular file, the screen read, 'Out of Order.'

223

I checked the troubleshooting guide in the manual but there's nothing like this in there."
(Show the owner's manual.)

It's Been Said

"Nothing is gained by winning an argument and losing a customer. "
—C.F. Norton

End by stating exactly what you want, and producing the warranty as you do so. "I want my money back," or, "I want the computer serviced with no additional cost to me," or, "I want a new computer."

If you present yourself calmly and professionally, and your paperwork is in good order, Melissa should accede to your request. If she doesn't, see the later section, "If All Else Fails…"

If you're a frequent customer and want to maintain a good relationship with the store employees, you should head over to Suzy Salesperson after the situation has been resolved. Tell her that you dealt with Melissa because you thought it would hasten the process and not waste Suzy's time. Suzy will understand—trust me.

Winning Without a Warranty

If you don't have the paperwork, or if your Smarto computer waits until the day after the warranty expires to break down (they usually do), you should still approach Melissa as I've described in the previous section. Since you don't have a receipt or warranty, your next best ally is the brochure or owner's manual that came with your computer (if you have it). Like most manuals, it probably brags about how durable, reliable, and easy the computer is to use.

If you've lost the brochure or owner's manual, ask for a replacement copy from the store before you approach the store about your complaint. Most stores have, or can get, a copy from the manufacturer.

Once you've got a copy of the brochure or owner's manual, you're ready to go in and discuss the problem. Quote all the highfalutin language in the owner's manual to Melissa Manager. If she's at all concerned with providing good customer service, she'll find it very difficult to refuse you. If she does argue, be prepared to equalize her statements:

Melissa Manager: "This computer looks worn out. Did you abuse it in any way?"

You: "I used the computer normally—only about an hour or two a night. That doesn't constitute heavy use."

Melissa Manager: "But your warranty has run out."

You: "The computer doesn't live up to the promises made in the brochure and owner's manual." (Quote any promises that relate to the longevity or dependability of the computer.)

Melissa Manager: "You don't have a receipt for this computer. I have no way of proving you bought it here."

You: "I bought it last year. You should still have a computerized record of the transaction, because I paid with a credit card." (Show the credit card statement if you have it. If you don't, you can probably order a copy from your credit card company.) Or: "Here's a copy of my canceled check, made out to Erratic Electronics." (Again, if you don't have a canceled check, you can order one from your bank.)

Dealmaking Tip
Respectable retailers are concerned about their reputation. Refunding or replacing your defective product will help promote the retailer's reputation. Don't hesitate to suggest that to the retailer.

If All Else Fails...

Most stores value customer satisfaction highly and won't hesitate to give you what you ask for: a refund, a replacement, or free repairs. Some will even throw in extra products or services to restore your faith in their product and company. But what if you face an obstinate employee who just won't give you any satisfaction? Here are some suggestions:

➤ Don't lose your cool in the store. You'll only give your opponent more reason to dig in his heels and refuse your requests.

➤ Try moving higher up the company ladder. If the store manager won't help you, try contacting the company president, by letter, if necessary. (Most executives take customer complaint letters very seriously and will route your letter to a person who has authority to deal with you.) Make sure you mention the model number, when you bought the product, and the location of the store from which you bought it. Include copies of any and all paperwork that documents your purchase.

➤ If you're still not satisfied, you may want to send a similar letter to the local Better Business Bureau, or your state's consumer affairs division. (You can find addresses for these organizations in your phone book.)

➤ If you feel strongly that a lawyer should be involved, you can contact an attorney and see if you have a case. Before you go this route, be sure to let the store manager and company president know that you are discussing the issue with a lawyer. This may motivate the dealer or manufacturer to give you what you want.

The Least You Need to Know

➤ Keep all receipts, warranties, and manuals that come with any product or service you buy.

➤ Make sure you fully understand the warranty before you buy a product or service.

➤ If you want a repair, replacement, or refund, ask the "yes" person for help.

➤ Be prepared to equalize every argument your opponent may raise.

➤ Use your opponent's written literature against him. That puts your opponent on the defensive and gives you the bargaining momentum.

Glossary

Arbitrator   A neutral third party who resolves a controversy between two or more parties.

Assumption   A negotiating technique in which you prompt a closing action.

BATNA (Best Alternative To a Negotiated Agreement)   The outcomes or alternatives that remain if no negotiated agreement is reached.

Bidding offer   The offer you make if you are bidding against other interested parties.

Body language   A series of gestures that reinforce or display what you are thinking, feeling, or saying verbally.

Brokers   People who are licensed to start and run their own real estate offices.

Building Block   A negotiating technique that permits you to parcel out facts during the negotiation so that they have a greater impact on your opponent.

Choice question   A negotiating technique meant to pin your opponent down to a definite course of action.

Closing   The process of finalizing all the dealings related to a negotiation.

Commercial real estate   Property used for a business, such as a restaurant or health food store.

Concessions   The compromises both you and your opponent are willing to make in order to reach a deal.

Conduit   A negotiating technique used when you are facing more than one opponent or you want to use your opponent to reach the "yes" person.

Contingencies   Events that must happen in order for a deal to close.

Controlled anger   A negotiating technique used to express your displeasure at something an opponent has said or done.

Counteroffer   A subsequent offer that makes changes to an original offer or counteroffer. Can be made by either opponent.

Dealbreaker   Any proposal, offer, or counteroffer that kills a deal.

Dealmaker   Any proposal, offer, or counteroffer that clinches a deal.

Earnest money   The down payment on a house.

Equalization   The ability to answer your opponent's argument with an equally compelling argument of your own.

Exhausting   A negotiating technique used to wear down your opponent.

Express warranty   An oral or written warranty given by a seller or a seller's associate.

Extrapolation   Stating facts in a manner that can only lead to one inescapable conclusion.

Funneling   Setting aside points once they are resolved. The points may be returned to later in the negotiation for review or summation, but not for renegotiation.

Gear Shifting   A negotiating technique in which you shift from issue to issue. It works best on large, complex negotiations.

General question   A broad question, best asked early in negotiation to uncover new facts and information.

Goodwill   The trust you build up with your opponent.

Highballing   Making an offer or counteroffer that is obviously too high for the negotiation.

Home field   Any place that you are intimately familiar with, such as your office or home; the best place for you to conduct a negotiation.

Implied warranty   A warranty that is not written but is assumed when you buy a product.

Investment real estate   Property you buy and hold on to in the hopes of eventually selling and making a profit.

It's a Shame   A negotiating technique best used when the negotiation is nearly settled and only a few points remain.

Jargon   The specialized language of a particular organization, occupation, or group.

Lawyer   A person licensed by the state in which he or she works to represent and advise people in legal issues.

Leading question   A statement turned into a question. Used to get an opponent to say "yes."

Lease   A contract that determines the rights and responsibilities of a renter and a property owner.

Lessee   A person who rents property from a property owner.

Lessor   A property owner who rents property.

Listed or asking price   A homeseller's offer for a house.

Lowballing   Making an offer or counteroffer that is obviously too low for the negotiation.

Manipulation   Using unfair or underhanded means to reach your goals.

Mediator   One who tries to resolve disputes between two or more parties.

Motivator   Anything that influences someone to act.

Negotiable offer   An offer that leaves room for wheeling and dealing.

Negotiation   A way to get what you want, deal with people, and increase your skills in human understanding and interaction.

Net rent   The money received after all the expenses associated with a business property are paid.

New elements   People, ideas, or issues that are foreign to the negotiators or the subject under negotiation.

Obvious question   A negotiating technique designed to get a favorable response from your opponent.

Offer   A proposal to pay, do, or give something such as money, goods, or services in return for other money, goods, or services.

Opponent   The person with whom you negotiate.

Option   In rental agreements, your right to renew a lease.

Personality   The distinctive individual qualities of a person, considered collectively.

Position paper   A written offer presented at the beginning of a negotiation.

Primary base   The most important issue you negotiate for; your objective or goal.

Principle   A fundamental truth or law upon which others are based; a rule of conduct; adherence to such rules; integrity.

Prompting Action   A negotiating technique that motivates your opponent to take a simple form of action that seals the deal.

Props   Any extra materials, documents, charts, or accessories you bring to the negotiating table.

Purchase agreement   An offer form used to make an offer to buy a house.

Salespeople or sales associates   People who represent property owners (usually sellers) and who handle the sale of a home or commercial or investment real estate.

Secondary bases   The positive factors that support your primary base.

Self-Deprecating   A negotiating technique in which you tactfully play down your merits or the merits of your bargaining positions. Used to form a bond with your opponent.

Specific question   A negotiating technique that calls for confined answers from your opponent.

Sublessee   One who rents property from another renter.

Sublessor   A renter who rents property to another.

Successive question   A negotiating technique used to maintain control of the negotiation and develop positive bargaining momentum.

Suggestive question   A negotiating technique that suggests a specific course of action.

Summarizing   A negotiating technique in which you summarize your understanding of the deal to prompt your opponent to say "yes" to it in its entirety.

Talk-Show Host   A negotiating technique used to uncover personal or private information from your opponent.

Vinegar and Honey   A negotiating technique used to make a bad negotiating situation or concession seem better than it really is.

Warranty   A written guarantee that goods or property will be repaired or replaced if not as represented.

"Yes" person   The person who has the authority to resolve the issue you are trying to negotiate.

Index

When You're Smart Enough to Know That You Don't Know It All

For all the ups and downs you're sure to encounter in life, The Complete Idiot's Guides give you down-to-earth answers and practical solutions.

Lifestyle

The Complete Idiot's Guide to Learning French on Your Own
ISBN: 0-02-861043-1 ▪ $16.95

The Complete Idiot's Guide to Dating
ISBN: 0-02-861052-0 ▪ $14.95

The Complete Idiot's Guide to Cooking Basics
ISBN: 1-56761-523-6 ▪ $16.99

The Complete Idiot's Guide to Hiking and Camping
ISBN: 0-02-861100-4 ▪ $16.95

The Complete Idiot's Guide to Learning Spanish on Your Own
ISBN: 0-02-861040-7 ▪ $16.95

The Complete Idiot's Guide to Gambling Like a Pro
ISBN: 0-02-861102-0 ▪ $16.95

The Complete Idiot's Guide to Choosing, Training, and Raising a Dog
ISBN: 0-02-861098-9 ▪ $16.95

You can handle it!

The Complete Idiot's Guide to Trouble-Free Car Care
ISBN: 0-02-861041-5 ▪ $16.95

The Complete Idiot's Guide to the Perfect Wedding
ISBN: 1-56761-532-5 ▪ $16.99

The Complete Idiot's Guide to Getting and Keeping Your Perfect Body
ISBN: 0-286105122 ▪ $16.99

The Complete Idiot's Guide to First Aid Basics
ISBN: 0-02-861099-7 ▪ $16.95

The Complete Idiot's Guide to the Perfect Vacation
ISBN: 1-56761-531-7 ▪ $14.99

The Complete Idiot's Guide to Trouble-Free Home Repair
ISBN: 0-02-861042-3 ▪ $16.95

The Complete Idiot's Guide to Getting into College
ISBN: 1-56761-508-2 ▪ $14.95

You can handle it!